Brando on Elvis

In His Own Words

Gary Lindberg

Minneapolis

Minneapolis

THIRD EDITION DECEMBER 2022

Brando on Elvis. Copyright © 2021 by Gary R. Lindberg.
All rights reserved.

No part of this book may be used or reproduced in any manner whatsoever without written permission except in the case of brief quotations used in critical articles and reviews. For information, write to Calumet Editions, 6800 France Avenue South, Suite 370, Edina, MN 55435.

BIO005000 Biography & Autobiography / Entertainment & Performing Arts

10 9 8 7 6 5 4 3
Cover and interior design: AuthorScope

ISBN: 978-1-959770-83-1

This book is dedicated with love to my sister Bonnie Lindberg,
who has encouraged me all my life

Table of Contents

Author's Note

Brando on Elvis consists of independent reporting and commentary about a collection of handwritten letters that appear to have been written by Elvis Presley, Marlon Brando, Harry Belafonte and Tom Jones. This book is not sponsored or endorsed by, and is not affiliated in any way with, the foregoing celebrities or their heirs and successors, including Priscilla Presley.

Also by Gary Lindberg

Nonfiction

Letters from Elvis

The Power of Positive Handwriting

(with Elayne V. Lindberg)

Historical Fiction

Ollie's Cloud

Thrillers

The Shekinah Legacy

Sons of Zadok

Deeper and Deeper

Brando on Elvis

In His Own Words

A Note from the Publisher

As a publisher, it is not my job to be a 'believer' of all the material contained in what we acquire, but to send out into the world titles which are earnestly written and honestly researched, in this case a title that carries the intention of prying free a hitherto buried truth: *Brando on Elvis: In His Own Words*.

After the mixed critical reception of Gary Lindberg's *Letters from Elvis* published by Calumet Editions in 2018, we felt the need to address one of the main complaints—that the verbatim content of the letters had not been printed. It didn't matter that a great deal of print space had been dedicated to explaining why that had not been done—fear of being sued, basically. It seems that certain responders, while taking the liberty to berate the author, did not bother to fully read the book. With a few exceptions, those who did read the entire book found themselves as engaged in the mystery as the author and his publisher.

So here, after asking for appropriate permissions with no responses, we have taken the risk of printing some of the actual letters Marlon Brando wrote to Carmen Montez. If Marlon's family or anyone else opposing the printing of these letters asks us to cease and desist we will have even more confirmation that the letters are genuine. So they're unlikely to make an overt objections.

There is no doubt that we must 'believe' that Brando's handwriting, now transcribed word for word into print, is authentic—

the authentication letter is printed in the pages of this book—but the question as to whether the reader believes what Brando and the others write is another issue. Author Gary Lindberg gives all the writers the benefit of the doubt and, lacking evidence to the contrary, responds to the letters as if they are reliable reporting of the events described. Is he being naive? You decide.

Brando on Elvis unfolds the unknown friendship of Marlon and Elvis, the startling subject matter of which has haunted the author for decades. I am pleased to be publishing the second title of what could be a lengthy series, all which will challenge the accepted history of the personalities involved.

Of course, as with *Letters from Elvis*, we will welcome interaction from readers who can shed light on the enigma of Carmen Montez and the whereabouts of her letters to these celebrities. Please reply to:

elvis@calumeteditions.com

-Ian Graham Leask, publisher, Calumet Editions

Introduction

Letters from Elvis ... and Marlon Brando

Shortly after publication of my book *Letters from Elvis* in November 2018, I received death threats. I expected some controversy but nothing like the insane explosion that occurred. One furious Elvis fan sent me a photo of my home, saying I would soon get a visit. I've since moved. I was accused of being a liar, a charlatan and an unscrupulous author looking to capitalize on Elvis's fame to make a quick buck. My publisher and I are still waiting for those imagined profits.

Of these irrational responders and reviewers, few had bothered to read the entire book and most had skipped the hundred-or-so pages describing the years of effort to verify the letters. Admittedly, the letters at the center of my book are strange and often at odds with the traditional histories of the letter writers. In some ways, they deflate the accepted stories about their lives. But if those 265 handwritten letters by six different individuals—some with postmarked envelopes—were somehow forged or fraudulent, the purpose of such a massive undertaking remains unknown since no attempt to profit from their creation has yet been made.

Letters from Elvis concluded with an appeal for a response from readers with information that might help solve some remaining mysteries. A gentleman from Utah, whom I shall call Brad, contacted me with startling news. He claimed to have another thirty-six letters from the same authors to the same recipient—plus some additional surprises. I will tell his astonishing story later, but he said my book had increased his appreciation for how Elvis had endured so many unknown tribulations. His words of gratitude, and those of many other thankful fans, helped ease the deep consternation I felt about being unjustly disparaged.

Of the many complaints I have received, the one that still haunts me is reader disappointment that I could not then provide verbatim transcripts of the correspondence in *Letters from Elvis*. Some accused me of not having genuine letters to back up my paraphrasing. Even though *Letters from Elvis* includes an entire chapter ("Legal Quicksand," pages 129-135) on the legal risks of publishing previously unpublished letters without author permission, many people were angry.

This book is a partial remedy.

The First Thirty Years

This remarkable journey began in 1988 when an artist friend, Bill Mack, asked me to help him untangle a book project that he was struggling to push forward. Bill, a collector of celebrity memorabilia, had invested in the publishing rights to a cache of 265 handwritten letters written by four entertainers who were friends and enormously popular in the 1960s and '70s—Harry Belafonte, Tom Jones, Marlon Brando, and the biggest star of all, Elvis Presley. Incredibly, all the letters were written to the same person, Carmen Montez, a woman who served as both confidante and spiritual advisor.

As an ordained minister in the Universal Church of the Master, the charismatic Montez had first established a business relationship with Belafonte, who in 1966 was grappling with painful marital, emotional and business issues. He found in Montez a sympathetic ear and a source of practical advice and spiritual support. Before long, Belafonte introduced Montez to his good friend, Marlon Brando, his compatriot in the civil rights movement, who also fell under the spell of Montez and developed a deeply confessional relationship with her.

Carmen Montez with her dog named Marlon.

Brando and Belafonte suddenly found themselves vying for the attentions of a young, beautiful and talented screenwriter, Joi Sommers, with whom Montez—an aspiring movie producer on the side—was promoting a film project. When Brando's friend Tom Jones met the captivating Joi Sommers, he instantly fell in love with her and began a trusting relationship with her mentor, Carmen Montez. The competition for Joi Sommers was ratcheting up, and Carmen's portfolio of influential acolytes was growing.

From the right, Harry Belafonte and friend Marlon Brando stand with author James Baldwin and actor Charlton Heston at the 1963 civil rights "March on Washington for Jobs and Freedom."

It was not long before Elvis Presley—another friend of Harry, Tom and Marlon—would be introduced to Montez, and he would become a close friend of Montez too, though they never met in person, only through correspondence. The four celebrities were prolific letter writers. Yes, even Elvis! Correspondence from Montez has not yet surfaced, but she saved many of the letters she received.

In early May of 1982, when Montez's best friend, Carmen Rayburn, learned that Montez had died of cancer without any heirs, Rayburn decided to attend the California auction of her friend's possessions. She bought a mirror, an assortment of other small objects and three unopened suitcases filled with "clothing." When she opened one of the suitcases at home, she found a heaped mass of letters and envelopes. The deeply-felt letters told true stories of love, friendship and loyalty as well as heartache, betrayal, kidnappings, murder and suicide attempts—none of which had ever been made public, and all of it described in the handwriting of the authors.

Immediately, Rayburn knew the letters could be the basis for an important and successful book, so she recruited an author and an investor. Bill Mack bought an interest in the book project and the author, Robert Slatzer, began work on a book proposal for publishers. But things didn't go well. Slatzer died, a morass of legal issues surfaced and Mack eventually sought my help (see, *Letters from Elvis*, Calumet Editions, 2018).

I recall my first reading of the letters and the emotions they stirred. The contents were so intimate, the passions and fears they communicated so vivid, the stories so sordid and incredible, that I wondered if the letters could be authentic. I was concerned about becoming the author of a book based on forged documents.

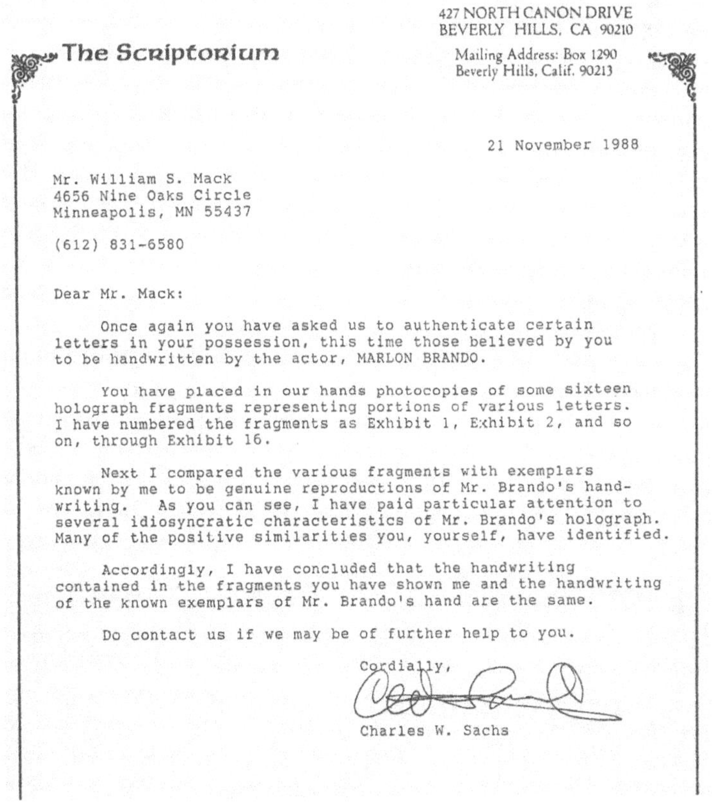

The Scriptorium

427 NORTH CANON DRIVE
BEVERLY HILLS, CA 90210

Mailing Address: Box 1290
Beverly Hills, Calif. 90213

21 November 1988

Mr. William S. Mack
4656 Nine Oaks Circle
Minneapolis, MN 55437

(612) 831-6580

Dear Mr. Mack:

Once again you have asked us to authenticate certain letters in your possession, this time those believed by you to be handwritten by the actor, MARLON BRANDO.

You have placed in our hands photocopies of some sixteen holograph fragments representing portions of various letters. I have numbered the fragments as Exhibit 1, Exhibit 2, and so on, through Exhibit 16.

Next I compared the various fragments with exemplars known by me to be genuine reproductions of Mr. Brando's handwriting. As you can see, I have paid particular attention to several idiosyncratic characteristics of Mr. Brando's holograph. Many of the positive similarities you, yourself, have identified.

Accordingly, I have concluded that the handwriting contained in the fragments you have shown me and the handwriting of the known exemplars of Mr. Brando's hand are the same.

Do contact us if we may be of further help to you.

Cordially,

Charles W. Sachs

The letter from renowned handwriting expert Charles W. Sachs authenticating the Brando script in the Montez letters.

In response to my skepticism, Mack hired a respected handwriting expert, Charles W. Sachs, to authenticate the letters. Sachs had gained worldwide notoriety as one of the authenticators who testified that the famous Howard Hughes handwritten will was not genuine, and his opinion was the cornerstone of the court's ruling against the will. Sachs stated that the Presley and Brando letters, which he examined, were indeed written by the respective celebrities.In all, the letters in Rayburn's collection were written in six completely different scripts. Numerous handwriting experts told me that even an expert forger could not convincingly duplicate the four celebrity handwriting samples. It would have taken at least four individual forgers—probably six—to produce such a collection of letters comprised of over a thousand handwritten pages.

Some of the envelopes were postmarked with dates consistent with the letters inside. Some experts told me that it could easily take a group of forgers many months, perhaps a year, to produce the quantity of handwritten documents in our possession. And for what purpose? Since the letters were written, no one has ever tried to profit from them.

Still unsatisfied that expert authentication might not be enough, I began fact-checking and cross-corroborating all the facts contained in the letters. If they were forged, errors would likely show up; letters often referred to events described in other letters and discrepancies could mean sloppy forging. Concert dates referenced could be checked for accuracy. Postmark locations and other geographic references could be checked against the historic record of each celebrity. I found almost no inaccuracies but did discover some information that could not be verified because neither corroborating nor contradictory data could be found.

Two roadblocks stood in the way of publishing the letters. First, the big New York publishing houses feared lawsuits by Elvis Presley Enterprises (EPE), which was notoriously litigious in defending against any intellectual property from which it did not make money or that might damage the value of its assets. Second, the copyright laws against the publishing of previously unpublished letters were both vague and punitive; in short, the laws state that the letter writer owns a copyright on letters he writes, and such letters may not be published without his (or his estate's) approval. Period.

These two unmovable obstacles appeared to doom the book project. Everyone associated with the book abandoned hope, but I continued to press on, hoping to find a hidden path to publication. By 2016, fate had led me to become involved in publishing, thus easing the first roadblock—provided I were bold enough to challenge the copyright laws and other legal complexities, such as rights to privacy. After much consulting with my business partners and several lawyers, we decided to go for it.

The second roadblock required some creativity. We decided to avoid the copyright issues altogether by not publishing the verbatim text of the letters. Instead, I carefully paraphrased the letters and used an abundance of other relevant content to fill in the cracks and provide context. The book, we decided, would also explain the thirty-year journey to our hoped-for publication of *Letters from Elvis*.

We hired a literary attorney to analyze my paraphrasing and advise on other legal matters. The resulting manuscript qualified for $2,000,000 of liability insurance, allowing us to move forward with printing. Our attorney sent out estoppel letters to all the letter writers and/or their agents, managers, heirs and estates. These estoppel letters explained our intent to publish a book based on the handwritten letters and offered to allow the writer or his representatives time to examine the letters, read the current draft of the proposed manuscript and file any suggestions or complaints prior to publication. The letters were sent by Certified mail—we have the receipts. Not a single recipient responded.

Gary Lindberg

April 19, 2018

By Federal Express

Re: **Calumet Editions**
The Elvis Letters
On-Press Date: August 1, 2018

Dear

On behalf of my client, Calumet Editions, I need to invite your attention to the following urgent matter.

Calumet Editions is publishing a book titled *The Elvis Letters.* The book will go on press on August 1, 2018, and will be published on September 1, 2018.

The book is based on a cache of handwritten letters that appear to have been written by Elvis Presley, Marlon Brando, Harry Belafonte and Tom Jones, and the book also makes reference to Priscilla Presley.

The letters in their entirety are not being published in the book. Rather, the author quotes selectively from the letters and is relying on the Fair Use Doctrine for the limited quotations that appear in the book. All use of the name, image and likeness of the various individuals in the book will be for editorial purposes only and <u>not</u> for advertising, merchandising or product endorsement.

The cover of the book will carry the following disclaimer: "This book is not affiliated with Elvis Presley, Marlon Brando, Harry Belafonte or Tom Jones." The following disclaimer will appear on an interior page.

Author Note

> *The Elvis Letters* consists of independent reporting and commentary about a collection of handwritten letters that appear to have been written by Elvis Presley, Marlon Brando, Harry Belafonte and Tom Jones. This book is not

Page 1 of the estoppel letter sent to multiple recipients.

sponsored or endorsed by, and is not affiliated in any way with, the foregoing celebrities or their heirs and successors.

Calumet Editions is offering you an opportunity to read and comment on the letters and the manuscript of the book prior to publication. If you wish to take advantage of the offer, I will send you a Non-Disclosure Agreement, and when it is signed and returned, I will provide a copy of the letters and the manuscript on a confidential basis.

As a practical matter, we will need to receive any comments you may have in advance of August 1, 2018, when the book will go on press.

We do not believe that any consent is required for the lawful publication of the book, but my client wants to extend this opportunity as a gesture of good will. However, out of an abundance of caution, I am obliged to reserve all rights on behalf of the author and publisher of *The Elvis Letters*.

Thank you for your prompt attention to this matter.

Sincerely yours.

cc: Calumet Editions

Page 2 of the estoppel letter.

On November 8, 2018, *Letters from Elvis* (after a slight title change) was launched at a Barnes & Noble in Edina, Minnesota. Over a hundred people attended, and the store ran out of chairs. The audience seemed stunned by the revelations in the letters, and we sold out the store's supply of books.

After the opening, I spoke about the letters at numerous bookstores in the region. I have posted large blown-up images of several letters to illustrate the differences in the handwriting and provide a colorful backdrop for my presentation. At a Barnes & Noble in Rochester, Minnesota, not far from the famed Mayo clinic, a reporter photographed me in front of these large handwriting samples. The next day, a photo and accompanying article appeared in the Rochester newspaper and immediately traveled to websites and social media accounts across the country. Before long, scores of amateur Elvis handwriting experts were doing their own fuzzy blow-ups of the newsprint photo and issuing countless homemade verdicts about authenticity.

Then the irrational controversy and dangerous abuse began.

The Controversy

As part of our effort to publicize the release of *Letters from Elvis*, we identified Presley fan clubs and other social media and message sites for advance notice of the book's release. To targeted individuals at these sites, we sent a PDF galley of the book's contents for review.

The first response came from an online forum comprised chiefly of collectors and traders of Elvis memorabilia, many of whom had become self-appointed experts in Elvis history. Several long-term members of the forum were widely seen by the rank-and-file as the enlightened ones and served as high priests—meaning *guardians*—of the conventional Elvis knowledge. I quickly learned that my book, and, by association with it, myself, were immediately perceived as direct threats to their Elvis fundamentalism. I had disrespectfully revealed startling new information that was unknown to them, exposing their façade of perfect knowledge. Worse yet, some of the information in my book contradicted longstanding and heartfelt beliefs about their idol.

Branding me an infidel, and with no honest debate, the forum members set out to vilify me in their forum and launch a campaign of negative reviews of the book on Amazon and elsewhere. I was astonished at the vitriol of their insults and the libelous charges of fraud. Here is a short sampling of the venom:

> The author writes "historical fiction" and this so-called expert's publishing company does not seem to have any presence on the net. This is either a bad joke or they need a mental health specialist.

I responded that yes, I have published historical fiction, but I considered his inference that *Letters from Elvis* was fiction to be malicious and deeply personal. Calumet Editions, my publishing company, at the time had a robust website listing scores of published authors and over a hundred books, so the forum member's facts were wrong, which called into question everything in his rant. I suggested that we should meet online and have an honest discussion.

Responding to assertions in handwritten letters by Elvis and Marlon Brando that Elvis had been raped, another member wrote in the forum:

> They lost me at the assertion of rape: that alone renders this project an absurdity. An incident such as this, if kept secret during his [Elvis's] lifetime would have been revealed after his death. Period, paragraph.

Absurd, really? Rape? When the assertion of rape is made by two well-known persons, one of which was the victim—Elvis Presley—I think it needs to be reported and investigated. The gang rape of Elvis is difficult to read about, but I'm sure it was even more difficult for him to endure. Blaming the victim (Elvis) or blaming the reporter (me) is hardly absurd as the critic asserted, especially in this #MeToo era.

The forum member seemed to believe that people like Elvis Presley and Marlon Brando cannot be victimized, that everything they do or endure somehow ends up in public view. I wonder if that member really believed that the Presley estate or Elvis Presley Enterprises would have allowed such information to be made public after his death.

Another forum member complained that my claim of having over sixty handwritten letters by Elvis violated "the established knowledge" of Elvis and his life. He wrote:

> It's a known fact that Elvis hardly wrote anything ... He was fully surrounded

> virtually every minute of every day of his life ... I think the author is disgusting.

By this time, I was getting used to being called a charlatan and disgusting. But this member's argument showed the problem of fundamentalism even in fandom. He was saying that I could not possess letters written by Elvis because "it's a known fact" that Elvis hardly wrote anything. That "fact" is one of the canons of Elvis fundamentalism—that because few examples of his writing have turned up, he must have not written very often. This suggests that the forum member believed Elvis could not easily write, and yet letters and cards by Elvis have surfaced and show no evidence that he had any difficulty writing cursive. I wish I could have asked this member how in his mind the "secret" letters written to a confidante might have turned up. Oh, yes, that's right… they did turn up, didn't they? Well, then, they must not be genuine. Imagine my frustration with such narrow-mindedness!

The Elvis fundamentalists have concocted a dogma about their idol, a major tenet of which is that Elvis "was fully surrounded virtually every minute of every day of his life." On its face, this is ridiculous, of course. Some of his entourage—the famed "Memphis Mafia" in particular, have made it sound as if they were so important that Elvis could not bear to be without their constant companionship and protection. The letters in my possession show this to be nonsense. And yet the obviously incorrect belief that Elvis was seldom alone is being used by this forum member to discredit the newly found facts that he *was* frequently alone, or at least without his usual companions.

To Elvis fundamentalists, any newly discovered information that contradicts traditional beliefs is despised, considered a threat to established doctrine, and branded heresy without proper investigation. Imagine if science operated this way. (Well, yes, there was that fellow named Galileo.)

Here is one final post by a forum member—there are scores of others, many unprintable:

> I understand people have to make a living. I just don't agree when they do so by taking advantage of gullible Elvis fans. Unfortunately, because of the nature of fandom, it's easy to find enough people that believe anything. History has proved that so-called "authors" have milked fans ever since august 1977.

The inference that I am one of those authors trying to make money off "gullible Elvis fans" is unfounded. The fact is that through my book, Elvis at last can directly speak to the public through his letters to Carmen Montez. Climate skeptics and letter-deniers notwithstanding, the letters exist and have been professionally authenticated. No one has proven their contents wrong, only that generally accepted but unproven assumptions about Elvis were often in error. The historical record is being corrected whether the self-proclaimed "experts" accept it or not.

A frequent charge against me is that I forged the documents myself or hired forgers to do so. Those making this charge believe that the handwriting analysis we commissioned was either fraudulent, incomplete or in error. Another common accusation is that I'm in cahoots with Graceland and Elvis Presley Enterprises (EPE), which couldn't be further from the truth. Others who have studied the letters, and agree with their authenticity, have been similarly, and falsely, charged. In today's culture it seems permissible to just make things up, to just say what they like, without evidence, say what they want to believe, and then somehow it gets into the accepted narrative—this is SO damaging. We MUST get back to following the evidence, which I am committed to doing as rigorously as possible.

To all these accusers I have made an offer that stands to this day. Any fan or researcher who wants to see the letters and is willing to bring along a credentialed handwriting expert to review them will be given access at my office, supplied with letters to analyze, and given as much time as necessary to be satisfied. The interested parties must pay for their travel and board since, so far, I have earned nothing from this book. Needless to say, no one has taken me up on this offer. Apparently, it is much easier to accuse than to stand behind one's accusations.

Did Marlon and Elvis Dislike Each Other?

Occasionally I hear this complaint from "experts" who have studied Elvis's history: "Your letters say that Elvis was a close friend of Marlon Brando and Tom Jones, but we know that they seldom saw each other, and then only professionally, so your letters cannot be true."

Well, of course I disagree, and there are pictures that show these individuals at the same photo session. Here are just a few. Study the two pictures below. Elvis and Marlon are at Marlon's Los Angeles home and are wearing the same shirt, sitting on the same sofa, being bugged by the same pesky cat, and pretending to work on the same typewriter.

Elvis at Marlon's Los Angeles home with a cat. This picture was taken for some unknown purpose.

Marlon at his home with the same typewriter on his lap, the same cat on his shoulders, sitting on the same sofa and wearing an identical shirt.

True, it is not widely known that Marlon Brando was a close friend of Elvis Presley. Photographs of the two have appeared in print, but because of harsh words about Elvis spoken years after writing to Carmen Montez, the popular notion is that the two men had met a few times but didn't like each other very much.

I have heard anecdotes about the Brando/Presley friendship from various sources, but the most convincing evidence of their tight bond in the late 1960s and early '70s can be found in the remarkable collection of handwritten letters Brando wrote to Carmen Montez. The traditional narrative is that Elvis considered Brando a monumental talent as an actor, something Elvis aspired to, and so the Memphis Mafia members and other staffers saw him as competition. They feared that Brando's domineering personality would vie for Elvis's affections.

As revealed in his letters to Carmen, Brando freely gave Elvis an abundance of advice on every aspect of his life—relationships with women, business affairs, health and safety, staff treacheries, acting tips, even the urgency of changing managers. But Elvis was not good at taking advice and increasingly pulled away from many of those who had tried to help him, including Brando. Undoubtedly feeling disregarded and scorned by Elvis, Brando eventually turned on his former buddy like a betrayed lover.

To quote from *Letters from Elvis*, Marlon was "suffering through his own crises—a suicidal daughter, a son convicted of murder, and career and financial setbacks" (*LFE* page 276). The fractured relationship between Elvis and Brando is what Elvis-watchers and fans remember. Their intimate but closely guarded relationship in former years became overshadowed by Brando's contemptuous verbal drubbing when he called Elvis a "bloated, over-the-hill, adolescent entertainer" in a 1979 Playboy interview.

Some of my readers believe this is proof that Marlon always despised Elvis. The stack of letters from these two men to Carmen say otherwise. I believe that Marlon wanted Elvis to change in certain ways, as he writes in his letters, but Elvis resisted and Marlon finally gave up, thinking Elvis a lost cause. The closer the friendship, the angrier and more painful the breakup.

Were Tom Jones and Elvis Presley Just Casual Acquaintances?

Some of my critics insist that Tom Jones and Elvis had only a professional relationship, not the deep affection portrayed in the Montez letters. Tom and Elvis greatly admired each other professionally, true, but consider these snapshots, which indicate that they were also comfortable just hanging out non-professionally, as their letters show.

Singer Tom Jones with his left arm around Patsy Presley, Elvis's double first cousin.

Tom Jones and Elvis jam at a casual home gathering.

Tom Jones and Elvis enjoy a private conversation.

Tom Jones and Elvis catching some rays in Las Vegas.

Marlon On Elvis

In the months following the release of *Letters from Elvis*, I have received numerous threats while logged into Facebook. The threats displayed as text messages and disappeared before I could capture the screen to report them. The language was sometimes unsettling but vague, like "May you rot in hell for trashing Elvis!!!" A few times, the message directly threatened me: "Your life is now officially over." I have already mentioned the unnerving photograph of my home. On Messenger, a Facebook user with the phony name of an Elvis relative told me that he was coming to my house the next day to tear me up. A woman with an Elvis Facebook page told me she was going to ruin my reputation among her legions of followers by exposing the "fraud" of my Elvis book. She followed this up with a litany of lies.

The Brando Letters and More

While the risk of publishing Elvis's verbatim letters is still far too great, Calumet Editions and I have decided to take the risk of publishing selected letters to Carmen Montez written by Marlon Brando. These are letters that refer to Elvis, describe situations in which Elvis was involved, or provide Brando's eyewitness accounts of Elvis's various relationships and encounters including brutal abductions.

The Brando letters are unedited for grammar and misspellings. They are verbatim transcripts of his handwritten letters to Carmen Montez. For readability, however, I have added some paragraphing because many of the letters were written as one long, unbroken paragraph. I also have added some annotations to provide needed context for each of the letters.

2
badly, but to answer ~~questions~~ questions
and be probed at by that kind of doctor.
It was a bad shock for him. It's
Caused him to run away for the weekend, alone, when he should have some
one with him. He's likely to keel over
at the wheel the same as he did
at the studio. The boy's anemic &
weak, not insane. But he's in the
perfect frame of mind to be driven
that way. El said not to worry, he
would be all right, & he'd be back Mon;
but nevertheless, I have worried.
Can't help it. This boy shouldn't be
driving. God go with him. I called the
residing Dr. in charge of the Bel-Air
hospital. He told me Elvis was suffering from exhaustion, coupled with a
deep & intense depression. Then I later
talked with Parker, at my party, after
Elvis left. He came to talk to me. He said
"Elvis is like my own boy (I doubt
it) but lately he's been way out, and if
he's sick he should have treatment."
Then he re-assured me he would
never expose Elvis to "that kind of

A page from a Brando letter showing the lack of paragraphing.

A month after *Letters from Elvis* was published, I located another thirty-six handwritten letters by these same four writers plus one by Priscilla Presley to Carmen Montez. The tale of how these letters came to be in Salt Lake City adds to the credibility of Carmen Montez and the trove of correspondence she received from Elvis and his friends.

The Brando Letters

April 3, 1967

The earliest Brando letter in my possession was written in 1967. The casual and familiar tone suggests, however, that other letters may have preceded it. This was an early clue that perhaps I did not have all the letters—after all, I had none of Montez's written replies—but I dared not hope that the missing correspondence would ever turn up. In a most astonishing way, however, it did. As promised, that story will be presented later.

As in many of Brando's confidential letters to Carmen Montez, this early letter shares his disdain for Elvis's wife, Priscilla, and the unceasing chaos of his own life. The "Tarita" he refers to is his third wife, Tarita Teriipaia, an actress of Chinese and French Polynesian descent who played opposite Brando in the 1962 film *Mutiny on the Bounty*. She was the mother of Brando's daughter Cheyenne and divorced Brando after ten years of marriage.

This letter reveals the marital tensions between Elvis and Priscilla, and the scene Brando describes in detail plays like a screwball comedy of the 1940s in which a group of inept conspirators attempts to gather incriminating evidence about Priscilla. As the letter reaches its conclusion, we learn a surprising fact about Priscilla that had never before been revealed.

Gary Lindberg

Dear Carmen,

What a nite! My wife broke her ankle, Priscilla took sleeping pills, Elvis fell apart! Two of my wife's three girl friends here share an apt. over at the Hollywood Towers, I later learned. Tarita called them and they asked around if any of their friends knew anyone in the building that Mrs. Presley ever visited. Loriella, the Tahitian girl, called Tarita back at 7:30 and told her that her girlfriend's boyfriend had seen her [Priscilla] visiting the divorced woman who lives next door to him [the boyfriend] on several occassions. Tarita told me "I don't care what you say about the girl, someone better try to do something. How is Elvis going to feel if anything does happen?"

She [Tarita] was all ready to get into the car with or without me. So we went down to her girlfriend's and the girlfriend called the manager, and the manager said the [divorced] woman in question was in Europe and no one was there. Then the boyfriend of my wife's girlfriend called and said the lights were on next door. So we all went down to his apartment. After a while we saw Priscilla standing on the balcony in back, then it got dark and my wife decided to climb out onto the balcony from this man's window. The balcony ran from the next-door apt. straight thru beneath the windows where we were, only on Priscilla's side there were French doors, and on ours only a window. My wife kicked off her shoes and came down barefoot on a planter that overturned and down she went and broke her ankle. I had to drop everything and take Tarita to the doctor and he said it is definitely broken and she has to stay at least overnight in the hospital, and they'll put on a cast tomorrow.

Then, when I got home Elvis called. He said he broke into the apt. where Priscilla was, and she had taken sleeping pills. Everybody in the building was there, he said, and someone had made her sick enough to get them up, and he'd called a doctor to be on the safe side, because she may have hurt the baby by it, or so he thought, and then he had called her parents to come and take her home with them. Then he started crying and crying like he was going completely to pieces.

He couldn't stop and he finally hung up. He was still shaking and couldn't talk when I got there. The doctor wanted to give him a sedative, but Elvis wouldn't allow it. Then Priscilla's parents came and there was a scene with her father and Elvis. I finally took Elvis' arm and just took him out of there. On the drive back he broke down all over again. He's in bad shape, Carmen, emotionally shook up, going to pieces inside. I made him stay at my place. With my wife in the hospital it was lonely anyway.

I made him go right into bed but I wonder if he's asleep. I doubt it. It's Elvis I'm sorry for. If Priscilla doesn't lose the baby in the next 24 hrs. she's probably alright, according to the doctor. But Elvis has had one deep hurt on top of another, and regardless how he feels about Priscilla now, on top of Jeni, and what happened there, it would be impossible for him to ever be the same. It would all come back, Jeni and everything, to eat away at him until it destroyed him. The only thing that can help Elvis now is love—the right kind of love—to make up for all this hell.

Well—I guess we all better say a few prayers.

Marlon

Elvis knows I'm his friend and I'm here and he can count on me but times like tonight—he needs a woman around.

Two points need clarifying here. First, in the sentence "It would all come back, Jeni and everything," Jeni refers to Elvis's greatest love, a woman whose disappearance caused Elvis great pain. He feared that she may have died. Brando believed she had not only passed away but was channeling messages to him from beyond the grave. Some of this channeled correspondence will be presented later.

Second, in the sentence "If Priscilla doesn't lose the baby in the next 24 hrs. she's probably alright," we learn that Priscilla was pregnant. Lisa Marie Presley, her daughter with Elvis, was born on February 1, 1968, and this letter was written April 3, 1968. Thus, shortly after giving birth to Lisa Marie, Priscilla apparently became pregnant again.

The casual way that Marlon tells Carmen "If Priscilla doesn't lose the baby" indicates that she also had prior knowledge of the pregnancy. It's usually the fifth week of pregnancy that a pregnant woman believes she may be with child. If we allow another three weeks or so for Priscilla to be properly diagnosed, she must have become pregnant with this child about February 1, 1968, the day Lisa Marie was born. This seems unlikely.

An alternative explanation is that Lisa Marie was actually born two months earlier than announced and the birth kept secret until exactly nine months after the wedding. (The precision of that nine months has always seemed suspicious to me.) This would mean that Priscilla became pregnant nine months earlier than that—let's say on March 1, 1967. That date, of course, is two months before Elvis and Priscilla were married. Is it possible that Priscilla was two months pregnant on her wedding day? We will probably never know.

The letters to Carmen Montez do not tell us what happened to this second child, but we have no evidence that a second baby was born after Lisa Marie. Perhaps the sleeping pills terminated the pregnancy as feared.

December 20, 1967

From these letters, it is obvious that Priscilla Presley and Marlon Brando disliked each other. Brando viewed Priscilla's childish behavior and disloyalty to Elvis contemptuously while Priscilla apparently saw Brando as a masculine competitor for Elvis's fealty. She feared the actor's growing influence over her husband.

Brando knew that Elvis had once loved a woman with such passion that he would never forget her. Jeni Pierson was a model who had appeared in a handful of national magazine ads. We don't know how long their relationship lasted or how it ended, but Jeni had disappeared, and Elvis feared that she might have died. He spent many years searching for her and even recorded a song with a coded message that he hoped she might hear and understand.

In this second letter to Carmen Montez, Brando describes a remarkable scene at a party that took place in Elvis's home shortly before he left for a grueling series of Las Vegas shows. Brando had gone into Elvis's large den to make a phone call, which did not go through, and so he sat in the shadows for a moment, retreating from the noise of the gathering. The scene he describes unfolds like a dream. It is difficult to take this story literally because a ghost suddenly appears in it. That this ghost was real to Marlon, however, is made clear by the presence of seven letters Marlon wrote to Carmen Montez in the handwriting of the ghost of Jeni who, in her words, was channeling her messages through Marlon. Several of these letters are presented later.

Gary Lindberg

Dear Carmen

I went to a party last night at Elvis' new place. It was a sort of Xmas-New Years and going away party because Priscilla wants to stay quiet she said from now until Feb.

I don't know, Carmen. I know now Elvis is no happier with her there, the way she's treating him, than he was without her. In fact, he looked very tired and the way he acted, I think he's ready to crack up. I tell you this because I don't know if you'll be able to help him when he goes so far away, and he really shouldn't be let to feel alone. I hope you'll go to him before he leaves. His wife has been taunting him by calling him some very nasty names every chance she gets. She started on him early in the evening last night. So, to spite her, he jumped up on top of the piano and started doing what I call the famous Presley "bedroom wiggle." Only the way he was doing it, he'd never get away doing it like that on the screen! How he can stand perfectly still and at the same time move all over is quite a trick. And that sarcastic smile on his face all the while. He got Priscilla as mad as a wet hen, which is why I know he was doing it. But he also got some of the women shook up, and later on two of them gave him trouble.

I'd gone into the den to use the phone and my line was busy, so I sat to wait in a big chair. When in came these two luscious blonde twin sisters, and did I get an ear full. I made a mental note to tell Elvis to keep away from their direction, when he came in to get some coffee for someone.

He poured the coffee and got to the middle of the room with his hands full when the two twins descended upon him. And I mean descended. They threw their arms around him, pulled the buttons off his shirt, even got him unzipped and the poor guy was standing there trying to keep from scalding anyone with the hot coffee, trying to reason with them to "act like ladies and cut it out," when, just as I was about to reveal myself, in walked Priscilla. She suddenly changed her use of words, but the new ones were just as bad. She turned and left and the girls fled in haste. Elvis threw down the coffee, cups and all and sank down in a chair in front of the desk. He put his head on the desk and I thought he'd cry his heart out then.

I was debating whether I should try to go and talk to him or stay back because I didn't want to embarrass him. Then I saw the girl, Jeni—in her blue dress. She was standing over him with her head very close to his. She looked like she wanted to reach out and put her arms around him, and just then she looked in my direction and our eyes met. She shook her head and I thought maybe I should just stay there quietly. After a while she disappeared.

When Elvis left, I left and came home. I'd hoped that when his wife came back, just maybe something would work out. But it doesn't look good and Elvis is a very miserable person. He's mixed up and confused. He's tried love and patience, and now he's rebelling, but it's himself he's spiting and hurting. Because this is not his nature. He loves what he wants this girl to be. But she's not what he wants her to be. If he could only see and accept that, and if she would meet' him halfway.

Priscilla is beautiful and she has a certain sweetness about her—but she's also spoiled, self-centered and stubborn. Elvis put her on a pedestal, but you can't love someone from there. The main thing I have against his wife is the way she closed her heart to him. What right does a sheltered 18-year-old girl who knows nothing of life have to judge him? She won't even let him explain. Even if it were the way she decided it was, any woman of warmth and maturity would consider and weigh the love he has given her and see the beauty that lies deep within him. If she really could see him, she wouldn't need to know any more. One day she will learn that a man who can be trusted is more rare than a thousand-dollar bill. So, if that's the way she wants it, I hope he can find his happiness elsewhere.

But I'm afraid he's going to brood and go on feeling miserable because it's losing Jeni all over again to him. And it's not really Priscilla that is driving him half out of his mind. It's his feeling of guilt over Jeni. And with this he is searching for something unknown. Something is lost, or never gained. But something is driving Elvis, and I'm most concerned.

For now,

Marlon

I'm sorry you won't be able to watch Elvis' picture on TV next Wed. He told me it was one of his best. "Roustabout." He said it gave him one of his best chances to act this far. In it he falls in love with an older woman. If I'm not mistaken it's Barbara Stanwyck. He said there were places where he had a very sad feeling and he thought he came across better than in the usual "little nothings" he usually does. I know he was hoping you'd get to see it but I know Wed. is your big night. He asked me if I would watch it with him and give him some pointers. So I'll see him at my place Wed. and I can give him your letter or message then. I feel it's progress that he asked me for help. At least he's trying. He has to make changes now or fade out. The kids he appealed to are no longer kids, and he's not wild enough for the kids of today, even though he looks younger than his age—I'm discounting the dance I saw him do last night when I say this!"

Jeni's astonishing appearance in the den implies that she had died and her "ghost" had attended the party perhaps as a response to Elvis's unceasing search for her. What makes this even more remarkable is Brando's matter-of-fact acceptance of this paranormal experience. He describes it and then quickly moves on, perhaps because a spiritual plane of existence is an accepted fact between he and Carmen. Clearly, Brando knew that Carmen would not be surprised by the appearance of Jeni's ghost at the party, so he described it as just another interesting anecdote.

I also learned that a function of Carmen Montez's ministry in the Universal Church of the Master was to serve as a medium—an intercessor between the living and the dead. Her faith believed not only in the immortality of the soul, but in the ability of the deceased to communicate with those who were still alive.

Brando mentions that Elvis's brooding is not entirely due to Priscilla's immature behavior, but also to his "guilt over Jeni." Brando writes that he feels miserable because "it's losing Jeni all over again to him." This may mean that his difficulties with Priscilla reminded him of issues he had with Jeni, and he is feeling guilty about not rising above the pettiness. The meaning is unclear, so readers must draw their own conclusions.

January 1968

Shortly after the pre-Christmas party, Brando wrote Carmen to wish her a Happy New Year and seized the opportunity to advise her on a business transaction. Harry Belafonte had introduced Carmen and her movie project to Brando hoping that the actor would agree to play a role, thus gifting the project with his star power and making it more fundable.

The introduction produced two deepening relationships. Brando adopted Carmen as his secret spiritual confidante, and he fell in love with Carmen's screenwriter/protégé who used the pen name Joi Sommers. Unfortunately, Belafonte was also in love with Joi, and Marlon's infatuation with the beautiful, young woman wedged open a divide between the two compatriots. Brando promptly gave Joi a nickname, Kit, perhaps as a way of staking a claim.

Two stunning revelations come out of this letter. As this correspondence occurs quite early in the relationship between Kit, Carmen and Brando, we can see the actor still denying his true feelings for Kit by stating that he imagines Kit to be a "candidate to fill Priscilla's shoes." This shows his concern for Elvis's happiness as well as his growing obsession with a woman many years his junior.

The letter also reveals that Brando believed in God, a belief that he will confess in other letters too. It is possible that he is just trying to build a bond with Carmen, the ordained minister, trying to make his words seem authentic. During this period, at least, Brando believed in the Almighty.

Dear Carmen

This is going to be very brief today because I'm between appointments. But Kitten sounded very discouraged when I talked to her, and I felt you were, too. And I don't want either of you to begin the new year feeling this way. Discouragement is our worst enemy. I can't tell your fortune or look into the future, but there are certain things about which I feel strongly.

One thing I feel is that Kit's new script will be the one to open doors. But I feel you both have to "move" on it without delay. I feel that somehow it is the will of God, or the fates, whatever that this go first. God wants you to do this for Him. In doing for Him you will gain your reward. There are no hitches in this—no actors, etc. to hold up things. And you know as well as I do, once you get one thing—just one thing on the screen—you can pretty well write your own ticket thereafter.

The other thing I feel about strongly is Elvis. Somehow, I feel an enlightenment about that situation. I'm not making predictions—but I do have a feeling. He needs you for his own personal sake. You could do worse than to have him for a friend. He's a loyal person to anyone who can get to him. Most people don't "get to him." And for some strange reason, I feel his marriage won't last long—and now, since he has had the try - since he did marry—he's going to need someone to love him. Someone who will take it slow with him, just be a friend—someone who will want and take what he has to offer—who needs a home and needs someone to need her and also needs a man she can depend on at the same time.

I'm not saying much, but I have an ideal candidate to fill Priscilla's shoes. And I think our spirit friend is for it because she's very unhappy because Elvis is unhappy. She looks a great deal like Kit. And strangely, lately Kit's been going towards more flowing clothes, towards a "newer" look—yet very feminine. She doesn't have to try to fit into Elvis' life. She is his type of girl. So, I feel, if you dedicate a portion of '68 toward this goal, towards doing for God—His script and His will—Carmen - perhaps He has His own will towards our direction. Everything points towards new goals—even for you. Once His will is done, I feel He will even allow you and Harry, and perhaps myself to all work together—but, did you ever think—perhaps it was not God's will for Kit and Harry to be together. It could have been for Jim, but when he proved worthless, we thought Kit and Harry would make it. But all the while, God may have had other plans.

And had you worked on this script with Harry now, it may have been disaster in their lives. But who is to say it is not in the future? Someday, you may know Harry well enough to sit down and talk to him. Both of him. He may be a different man, you may be in a different position. Things can change in a moment's notice. So now, ask God's guidance and go forward for Him. As Elvis says, this is one who never lets you down.

Harry has to stay away from Kit while she's upset, because he's in no condition for upset. Perhaps this, too, is part of the master plan. I have great ideas for this new script. I want to sit down one day before I leave and tell them to you and get your reaction. Elvis is ready to do better things and perhaps already this idea has been planted in his mind. When I start on the script, I'll let you put a few ideas in his head. I feel you will know him before it's finished. I'll write before I leave.

Have a Happy and prosperous New Year and you know my wishes for you and for Kitten.

Love, Marlon

At first, I was confused by Marlon's handwritten words, "When I started on the script…" I knew that Joi had written a screenplay that Belafonte recommended to his good friend Marlon Brando. But suddenly a different script seemed to have surfaced, one that Brando was authoring. Later I learned that Marlon had offered to barter his participation in a movie project to Carmen and Joi provided they agreed to switch their focus to a different screenplay that he was writing. For upstart producer Carmen Montez and new writer "Kit," this opportunity seems to have been too good to pass up. Carmen could get a producer credit, and Joi could work with a bonafide movie star on refining a screenplay.

March-April 1968

According to the letters in my possession, between two and three months passed before Brando again wrote to Carmen Montez. But clearly, the smooth-sailing relationship has run onto some rocky shoals.

In this letter, written by Brando sometime during March and April, 1968, Marlon explains why he wrote the screenplay *Let There Be Light*. It also suggests that the movie project has caused a rift between the foursome—Carmen, "Kit," Harry and Marlon. I suspect that Harry—who could be as opinionated and domineering as Brando—had taken issue with Marlon hijacking a project to which Harry felt some ownership. Nothing is more central to a movie deal than the script, which had now been replaced by Marlon's work—work which so far has not been located.

In *Letters from Elvis* (pages 163-174), I explain many details about a love affair between Joi Sommers and Harry Belafonte's secret half-brother Jim Matthews, who was unreliable in love and business, leaving Joi with a child that both Harry and Marlon helped support. In this letter, Brando refers to "Jim" for the first time.

Dear Carmen

I have waited until the very last moment to hear from you regarding the business proposal, etc. I can wait no longer. I'm

forced to leave the situation in my sister's hands and since I doubt her business capabilities I will probably disband the corporation I intended to form. I am very lucky in business matters. This year I seem to have lost all that has been dear to me for a major portion of my life. I have felt an influence working, even attempting to undermine our own friendship. I have fought against this with all my power, trying to aid Kit in her need and trying to help you, even though sometimes it has been merely through advice. I have fought because I know our goals have been, I should say are wrapped up in one another.

We all desire to strive to be successful. This is human nature. But in our case, at least I always felt—our true desires were more than just money and praise. Our goal, which I believe was mutual - was far deeper, and it involved the happiness and togetherness of others. When I wrote the script "Light" it was for reasons other than personal acclaim. If I had wanted that the most, I could have produced it myself. But I wanted it to come from you, from Harry, from Kit. Each person's own efforts to be his own reward, and my own award then from this achievement. I never have given up faith that this would still be, although not exactly as we had envisioned at the time. We each have to do other things, to live our own lives, but if we each succeeded independently, then in our success we have been defeated. our mutual togetherness is the only real goal where I am concerned.

"Light" is not the only answer to this goal. And if it has rendered us apart, then it is to my regret that I ever had this dream. I believe, Carmen, first of all in racial equality. Secondly, I believe in our own individual talents. I believe Harry is one of the most gifted people today. His gift is inner understanding. And I believe he can prove himself as an actor. I believe Kit has great creative talent, a sense of timing and ability to pick up, describe and keep a situation moving, even to the point of direction. I don't know too much about you in the category of direction, but I feel your greatest talent lies in being able to "put together", to see into the heart of things; to put together not only a production package, but to bring together the people, the right people, the right elements for an understanding of what we are basically trying to do. And what we are trying to do, or at least what I am trying to do is bring about a betterment to this sorry old world, whether it be thru racial understanding, spiritual understanding and enlightenment—and this need not come thru any one script, important as one may be. This should be the goal of our lives, not of one effect in our lives.

And I believe with a determination, without a doubt our lives are and always have been bound together, in all time, all worlds—yours and mine, Harry's, Kit's, Jim's—even this child, and my Chris. And once this tie is torn, we will not succeed, not in heart—in this life or any other. I hope I have not offended you in any manner, but I do wish you would have contacted me. If you even want me, I will be in touch with Kit. My plane leaves at midnight and I don't know if I shall be back in a week or a year. It matters not to me at this time.

Wishing you success in your desires,

Marlon

P.S.

One thing I have to tell you about before I leave. I expect my wife to contact you. She has tried to pull something on Kit and I and it is still pending because of the new turn regarding my illness. She told her lawyer she doesn't know Kit but knows she is someone I am seeing. One day a couple of weeks ago she brought you up, "Kit's friend Carmen", and said I'd given money to you and she had given money to you. Basically, my wife has many good points, but she has often had flare-ups of jealousy and then she's not the same person. The day after she said these things, I figured she was calm and I asked her about them. She then said she didn't know what I was talking about and she didn't know you. So if she contacts you, I think it will be wiser for your sake as well as mine to just tell her you are in this business and you know many actors; neither admit nor deny you know me. It may not be a good thing to admit it, and if you deny it she may have some way of proving differently. She may have a letter or card from you to me as your husband had from me to you. I've always tried to be very careful. It was partly for this reason I didn't want scripts around my home. She may come to you sweetly and want to cry on your shoulder about me, or she play it sly and want to ask you questions about me, or she may be bitchy. This I doubt, but she is under the influence and advice of another man, so I don't know what she may do.

At any rate I don't want to involve you and I hope she doesn't try it because it will make me very angry if she does. Thank you. I found my Easter card and Harry's still at Kit's. I know it's late now, but they are yours, so I want you to have them regardless. I know Kit had bought one for you weeks before Easter, because I gave her the money, and she also told me Tony sent one for you enclosed in hers, but I can't find them right off. They're at Kit's somewhere, so don't think Tony forgot.

When Brando refers to "my Chris," he means his son Christian Brando, one of eleven children and the product of an affair with actress Anna Kashfi. Christian was ten years old when this letter was written. Twenty-two years later, Christian shot and killed Dag Drollett, the boyfriend of his half-sister, Cheyenne, in Marlon's home on Mulholland Drive. He pled guilty to manslaughter and served six years of a ten-year sentence. A year before Christian's release, Cheyenne Brando committed suicide by hanging herself at her mother's home in Tahiti. Christian died in 2008 after twelve years working as a tree-cutter and welder. Personal difficulties, like the ones to which Marlon alludes in this letter, continued all his life.

July 1968

By July 1968, Brando seems to have patched up his relationship with Harry, Carmen and Joi. In this letter to Carmen, he reports that Elvis has become deeply depressed and ill after watching the movie adaptation of Tennessee Williams's play *Suddenly, Last Summer*, which ends with a revelation about cannibalism.

Dear Carmen;

Well, I really goofed last night with Elvis! I feel bad about it because I've been trying so hard to pull him out of this. He won't come out of this shell he's drawn into. El's got Tom Yohotam coming in days, and living out because there's no room in the house for him. So, I got the bright idea that after I get paid for this picture, by Xmas time, El and I can share Tom and Tom can stay here for a while until El gets resituated and maybe gets a bigger house.

So I went over and talked to both of them, and Tom and Elvis were each agreeable, and Tom made a nice dinner for me to celebrate. I had intended to go home and watch the Tennessee Williams movie [*BOOM!*], because I really dig Tennessee Williams. Next to Shakespeare, you know. Since eating there made it late, I asked Elvis if I could watch it there. He hasn't been watching television or doing anything Carmen. Just listening to church music and brooding. Tom had brought the dinner to Elvis' room, so he couldn't refuse. And honestly, Carmen, I did not know what that picture was all about. I thought anything, even watching a little T.V. would do Elvis good. Even then I couldn't guess the ending.

If you've seen "Suddenly Last Summer" you know what I mean. I thought the cousin had murdered the boy, or even the mother to cover up something, but I couldn't figure it as it was. Only Tennessee Williams could come up with something like that [cannibalism]. I'm telling you, Elvis turned all shades of green. He flew out of the bed and into the bathroom and he was terribly upset. Finally, I told him I was going to stay with him because he looked like he was ready to keel over. He'd actually become physically sick. He didn't want me to stay, I knew. But I was really upset myself Carmen. I think he knew I didn't do that on purpose. I wasn't trying to jolt him into anything. He said he knew, but I hope he really does believe me. I'd never subjected him to such a psychological experience as that.

My staying with him didn't help much, though, because he spent most of the night in the bathroom, and finally when I got up, he was asleep on the couch in the living room. He said he was embarrassed for reacting so strongly, but I quite understand. Besides that, this time of year is a bad time for Elvis. I think it's about now when he lost his mother and his girl could kick myself from here to Europe and back, Carmen. Everything I try to do turns out wrong, and I just don't know what I can do. Please say some special prayers for him. The poor kids all mixed up and I really pity him.

Harry sends love. He's fair and will be with me tomorrow. He probably will be unable to read or write but I'll give him your love.

Marlon

It's interesting that Tennessee Williams, author of the play on which the film *Suddenly, Last Summer* was based, told the *Village Voice* in 1973 that the screenplay strayed too far from his original work and "made [him] throw up."

When Marlon wrote in this July letter "I think it's about now when he lost his mother," he is rounding off. Gladys Presley, Elvis's mother, died on August 15, 1958.

Late August 1968

On August 28, Elvis finished his role in the movie *Charro!* He returned to his home at 1174 Hillcrest Drive in Beverly Hills for a couple days with plans for driving to his Palm springs home with Priscilla to recuperate. Unfortunately, as he was backing out of the driveway, he struck Priscilla, who was pregnant again. The baby was lost.

In the details of a letter to Carmen Montez, reported in *Letters from Elvis* (pages 138-140), he expresses the trauma of feeling responsible for the death of his own child. Priscilla quickly left for Memphis to heal, leaving only Gene Smith, Elvis's cousin, at the house with Elvis until Marlon Brando arrives to spend the night and comfort the grieving performer.

This letter presents another paranormal experience. After going to sleep, both Elvis and Marlon had nightmares. Elvis woke up screaming because of the frightening vision of someone trying to slip a rope around his neck. Marlon had trouble sleeping afterward because Elvis kept moaning and calling out for Carmen. Suddenly, Marlon detected a strange sign of Carmen's presence in the house, as if the spiritualist had answered Elvis's call. To a skeptical reader, this paranormal experience may seem like gaslighting or pandering to his dear friend Carmen, the spiritualist, but to me this report seems in keeping with his belief in ghosts and other related phenomena. Whether real or imagined, I think Brando experienced this phantosmia and described it as best he could.

Gary Lindberg

Dear Carmen:

I'm still very worried over our boy. He seems very restless, very haunted. He wanted so much to write to you today, and he just couldn't make it. He finally tore up the paper and put his head down on the desk. He was frustrated and deeply disturbed. And tonight, his first night alone in his own house (alone except for Gene) he's not sleeping. We made him get into bed, but he couldn't eat anything. He's lost 11 lbs. and Tom won't be there until Thurs. now.

Later on I came back to see how he was doing before I went to sleep. He wasn't in his room. I finally found him standing in front of the kitchen sink. He was staring at an open drawer with a neat row of knives in it. I watched him for a minute then called him before he could make any move. The minute he saw me he swung around and said "I wasn't doing anything" like a kid caught in a cookie jar. Right there his quick response betrayed the guilt of temptation.

The next instant his face changed, started to twist like someone in unbearable pain. I tried to take his arm to help him back to the bedroom, but he only clenched his mouth and shook his head and couldn't seem to say anything at the moment. I asked him if he wanted to come back to my place for the night. He shook his head and said he was "on his own" now. I'm not sure he's ready for it yet. He's been too alone for too long.

At my place the days were long with too much time to think glum thoughts, but there was a certain protection there. He knew we were close by, that we cared. He still knows it, of course, but it's somehow different over there. I didn't want him to watch that picture last night. I didn't think it was good for him. I tried everything to distract him. I tried to get him to get up and come to the kitchen with me. In desperation I made some hot chocolate and brought it in to him and tried to chatter him to distraction. I got shushed for my trouble and while he drank the chocolate it could have just as well have been a cup of brown ink for all he knew.

Finally, when "Jailhouse Rock" was on about 15 or 20 minutes, Elvis remarked "you know, that's something I'd never do." I said "What?" and he answered "pills, women are such cowards!" So, it was still on his mind, and it disturbed me so I had bad dreams. In mine you and I were chasing two mice with of all things butterfly nets! You were helping me hunt the creatures, and we were crawling around under furniture and all over the place! Crazy? I was· awakened from that by a yell from Elvis. I flew to his room and turned on the light and he was sitting up in bed and swore he'd seen a figure in black standing by his bed trying to get a rope around his neck. By the time I convinced him he was dreaming I was more than willing to go back to the mice!

I tried to go back to sleep there, but Elvis who usually is the world's most quiet sleeper, moaned in his sleep, called to you, and turned from side to side until daylight. Then about that time your powerful perfume came drifting over and I knew we had company. So I sneaked back to the guest room and got about an hours sleep before the phone rang. So I gave up!

But Elvis is definitely a disturbed, mixed up young man for all his attempts of restraint and apathy and display of a lack of emotion. When he's alone he settles back to his old thoughts. When he thinks anyone is watching, even me, his guard goes up. He can't seem to help it. He's kept himself fenced in for so many years he lives with an iron fence and gate around his soul. But tonight he almost broke, the gate was cracking. But he locked it just in time. I was watching him very closely in the movie last night—shaking up a storm and doing it all with the most innocent face you could ever see.

And I took a good look at Elvis sitting there. He still has a certain innocence in his face. And his face hasn't a line to betray a dozen years of hell. And yet it's there—a deep sadness starting to show in his face, and it's impossible to define what brings it to the surface, only that it's there. I guess I try to crawl inside people too much. The old method actor again!

All I know is Elvis needs someone with whom he can be at ease—say and do as he must—and he needs it badly. I can help, but I can't take this thing out of him. And I feel so bad. That's life, I guess.

Marlon

Brando's compassion for his friend shows a side of his personality that few people have mentioned. Was this bond created by the various personal and family traumas each were attempting to endure? If so, the bond was due to grow even stronger.

September 7, 1968

The historical record states that after shooting *Charro!* Elvis traveled to his home in Palm Springs to rest for most of the month. That may have been his intent, but according to Elvis's own account, the tragic loss of a child changed that plan. If he did go to Palm Springs for a time following that incident, it was a short-lived visit. From this letter, we now know that Elvis came back to Los Angeles for several days to complete a project with Brando.

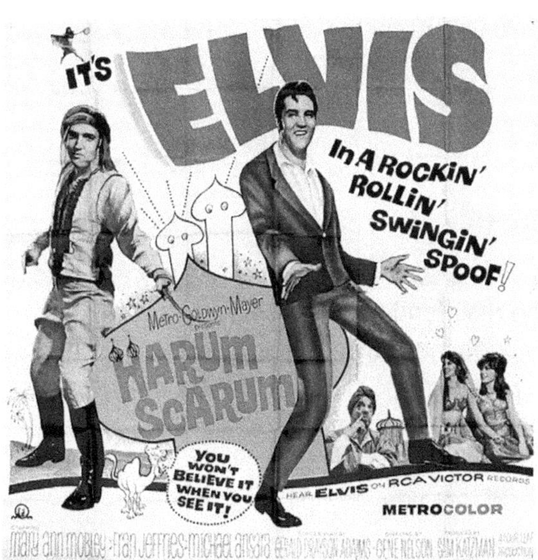

Harum Scarum was produced by Elvis's tormenter Sam Katzman.

Some background information is essential here. If you have read *Letters from Elvis* (pages 190-196,) you know that B-movie producer Sam Katzman and Elvis were engaged in a longstanding feud. Sam Katzman had produced two terrible Elvis movies, *Kissin' Cousins* (1964) and *Harum Scarum* (1965). Three years later, Sam Katzman deployed a gang of thugs, including two Katzman relatives, to abduct and torture Elvis.

This letter from Marlon Brando to Carmen is like a scene from a buddy movie about two average Joes who are moving stuff from one house to another with a pick-up. Can you imagine Elvis Presley and Marlon Brando hauling boxes in a truck? Maybe this is what celebrities do when no one is watching—act like normal people.

The domestic drama plays out as expected for a time, but then takes a shocking turn into Sam Katzman horror-movie territory when Elvis and Marlon are both abducted at gunpoint. Brando's reporting of this incident is strange and disjointed, what a reader might expect from someone reliving a traumatic experience shortly after it occurred. The abundance of detail—some of it perhaps distorted by Brando's shock—may demonstrate an attempt to reconstruct the specifics before losing them to fading memory.

Dear Carmen:

This is a very desperate situation. And since we are the only ones who really and truly realize and know the danger. It falls into our hands for the decisions. It is a very grave thing because Elvis is in the clutches of a band of vicious homos who more resemble animals than anything human, and even if we know where Elvis was, nothing short of a squad of Police could free him.

I'm so afraid of what they've done to him, and I'm afraid because I don't know how we can handle Elvis when we do get to him. And only you and I will be able to do anything there. I'm trying to protect him from the scandal that would make his life unbearable. But in doing this I may be prolonging hours of agony he will have to endure. Elvis is moving out of the house on Rocco and I was helping him move some of his things over to the Trousdale house, and since I hope to go back to Europe again, I let him store some things in my house until he can get himself straightened away and situated. Pris is gone again and there are things he doesn't want her to get her hands on his mother's things, etc. Tom [Yokohama] is on the second week of a three-week vacation and Saturday some of Elvis' buddies were going to help in the morning but Friday it was just the two of us.

We had made three trips back and forth in two Pick-up trucks and we were getting ready to take a lunch break when we came back from the last trip. There was a sudden noise outside, shouting and horns tooting and a sound like rocks hitting the side of the house close by the dining room window. El went to look out the window and I was close behind him.

We saw two strange Caddies inside the driveway and just as I turned away from the window something hit me like a ton of bricks. It took us so unaware, and before we could make a move, Sol Katzman's brother and some other guy had stepped out from behind the long curtains and beat Elvis at his own trick with a series of rapid karate chops that served to paralyze our nerves for several minutes. Elvis came out of it first, and when he straightened up and turned around, Katzman (the one El and I fought last year) ordered Elvis to "lie down on the floor". He said he was going to whip Elvis, he'd waited for the chance since the fight last year. He took a leather thong whip out of his pocket.

Elvis said, "they'd have to make him get down." He never would bend to them willingly. Whereupon Katzman told the other guy to hold his gun behind my ear. I was still semi-paralyzed from the effect of the karate. Elvis looked at me and I could see him getting sick inside. Katzman had by now eyed Elvis' big silver belt buckle and now ordered him to take off the belt and his shirt. That buckle could cut him to pieces. They used me to force him. Because of me he pulled out the shirt and got down on his knees but before he got to the belt, Sol Katzman and two other guys had come in through a window in the kitchen.

Sol Katzman said "No, I don't want him beaten—just yet." He ordered Elvis to get up. He got up and tucked in his shirt and saw the gun was still on me. I'd been waiting my chance to make a move and now with five against us, it was too late. Katzman ordered Elvis to go to the bathroom and shave off the beard he'd grown for the picture. The other two guys went with him. They had guns also. If it weren't that it was an electric razor, I think Elvis would have cut his throat then and there.

Making him shave is one of the weird aspects to this thing. When he came out, they took the leather thongs from the whip and tied one around each of his wrists and then knotted the two together. Sol Katzman then forced him to drink about 2 oz. of a clear liquid from a small bottle. I don't know what it was. Elvis obviously didn't like it. He looked at me hard—Elvis. I think he was trying to tell me something; maybe to get to you, the only one who's ever been able to rescue him from a tight Place before.

Then they shoved us out with the gun still at my head and Elvis had to go with them because of me. He had no chance Carmen. They forced him in the back seat of one of the Caddies with Sol Katzman and his two friends. and I was shoved in the front between the brother and his friend with the gun. They drove up to my place, made me get out and that's the last I saw of Elvis. I just got a fast look at him when they shoved me out. His eyes held that pleading look yet and he was very white and drained even under the tan.

They made me unlock my door, shoved me in a closet in my soundproof bongo room, hit me on the back of the head with the gun barrel and locked me in the closet. When I came to, I was tied up with my tie and my handkerchief was tied over my mouth.

By the time I got free and managed to get the pins out of the door about three hours had gone by. When I couldn't get Kit to get you, I tried to reach Gigi ["GeeGee" Gambill, Jr., who is the husband of Elvis's first cousin Patsy Presley.] They're off to Vegas for the weekend and the Fortas brother who is Elvis' buddy is also out of town. I've to get a private detective friend of mine to help, but he wouldn't go for the involvement.

I don't know what they are capable of doing, or how far they will go. I can't think the way such a sick mind would think. The second Cady followed us, and I think all in all there's about eight of them against one man. They're maniacs and even if they don't mean to kill him, anything could happen. What can I do even when we reach Elvis? They're brazen, they don't care. They know there's too many of them. I can't imagine how they could hope to go unpunished and they don't seem to care. "Uncle Sam" [producer Sam Katzman] is not home. They knew everybody close to Elvis was out of town. I don't believe they expected me.

Just in closing—El changed his blue shirt for a white one and he had on black levis, the leather belt with the big silver buckle, and short black boots. Please help me if you can. He might not have been in this situation if it weren't for me. At least he'd have had a chance. I'm hurrying now, but please tell me what to do. I'm frantic.

Marlon

Brando was clearly a co-victim of this brutal abduction, more intimately involved than merely an eyewitness. Marvin "GeeGee"

Gambill, Jr., was a longtime friend of Elvis Presley and a member of his personal staff in the 1960s. He and his wife Patsy, Elvis's double first cousin, divorced, and he died on February 20, 2005 after being struck by a vehicle as he walked to work in Nashville.

"GeeGee" Gambill with his wife Patsy (left) and Priscilla Presley (right).

September 7 or 8, 1968

Before Marlon heard back from Carmen, he fired off another letter. In this and subsequent letters, Marlon provides details about the results of the Katzman gang's torture as he understands them. We must keep in mind, however, that Marlon is not a medical professional and likely is mishearing or misinterpreting some of the medical information. Reported by Marlon in layperson's language, these facts cannot be taken as medically accurate.

Elvis also provides many details of the abduction and torture to Carmen, but not until a few months later. It seems that he needs to get some distance from the event before he can put his experience into words for his female confidante. These details can be found in *Letters from Elvis* (pages 202-220.)

Marlon's comment that "this thing is going to be very hard on Elvis where women are concerned. He's going to need guidance to get himself straightened out," is confusing at first. I believe that Marlon is alluding to the circumstances of the abuse Elvis endured, much of which was sexual in nature and perpetrated by males. Like many men of his era, Elvis worried that he might be partially responsible for these acts because of some innate homosexual tendencies—"signals" the rapists may have picked up and acted upon. I wonder how Brando would have felt about this in light of his later revelation that he was bisexual.

In this letter, Marlon provides the only testimony to Elvis having a sinus condition, a possible consequence of some unreported torture inflicted by the Katzman gang.

Dear Carmen;

I'm still deeply perplexed as I await your letter. Elvis was sitting up a little today, just starting to mend physically after one week of misery. Mentally and spiritually he is far from mending, though. He's breathing easier but has nothing to say. Part of his breathing difficulty was discovered yesterday when they took X-rays of his head for the first time. He had been severely burned inside the nose and up into his head, and the sinuses had become blocked. I guess Elvis was—and is—in too much of a daze to know what bothers him in particular. He must be one big ache.

Psychologically this thing is going to be very hard on Elvis where women are concerned. He's going to need guidance to get himself straightened out. It's really going to be rough on him. I guess I feel so personally involved in this thing because I was used as the pawn to get at Elvis. It goes against every principle I know to let them get away with it, but at the same time it would be very difficult for me to live with myself if through me Elvis had to suffer any more pain and misery.

This is one time that I really wish you could foresee the future and tell me what is to be done. Well—meanwhile—even though we're all concerned—keep things going with the script. It now seems the only door to open to get to Elvis, and he's going to need help by the quickest route anyone can travel. Even if the script itself should fail, it has to serve its purpose as the key to this-closed door. And if it does that much and no more, I will be happy to have had part in it. I hope it is accepted as a good property. I'm personally curious to the reaction. I dreamed with Jeni the other night, and she said in the dream to not worry about content, she would fix that. I wish she could fix a few other things.

Well, I'll close until I hear from you.

Marlon

P.S. I guess you probably have the meeting with Doug Lawrence [producer of Elvis movies *Speedway* and *Stay Away, Joe*] next week. Start working on Peter Tewksbury [director of Elvis movies *Stay Away, Joe* and *The Trouble with Girls*] right now. This time, lay the ground plans out ahead of time between Lawrence and Tewksbury and you should make it!

By the way, the girl I found and helped, Maurishka, who was in "Joe" [*Stay Away, Joe*] is getting a big build-up. She's Miss Press Club of the Year, was a judge on the Miss America Pageant and is being billed as an "international star." I pick 'em, don't I?

The sudden shift from a deeply personal lament about Elvis's mental and spiritual health to a business discussion regarding the movie script that Brando is helping Carmen develop demonstrates how business and career interests dominate the attention of Brando. I suspect Brando knew these interests were constantly on the mind of Carmen Montez as well, so it probably seemed natural rather than absurd for Brando to jump from one topic to another.

Maurishka Taliaferro, referred to in the postscript, was an exotic and sought-after model in the 1960s. She used her popularity to gain a role on her favorite TV series of the time, *Star Trek*, of which she was a huge fan. Besides appearing with Elvis in *Stay Away, Joe*, she had an uncredited role with Fred Astaire in the film *Finian's Rainbow*.

September 9, 1968

The Katzman gang, which behaved with a sense of invincibility, appears to have had second thoughts about the possible consequences of kidnapping and torturing a man of Elvis's celebrity. According to this letter by Marlon Brando, Sam Katzman or some gang members began threatening Marlon to keep quiet about the event.

Dear Carmen:

I had a terrible phone call today concerning Elvis and I am terribly in need of advice. I know who it was and they're probably shaking in their boots now. The voice said I'd better keep my mouth shut tight and make no moves or El would die. "You won't know where or when," he said, "but it's going to be nice and slow and we'll let you watch."

The trouble is, it isn't just the two we know. There were eight others and we don't know who they are. That is their cover, their reason for their boldness. El's only weapon is to cover himself at all times with someone around him. Someone who can handle a gun real fast. Still, he can't drag a dozen guns around with him wherever he goes I think that's one reason he doesn't go many places ever.

He lives so to himself. I feel sick to my stomach after that guy called me. He knows if I think enough of Elvis to get mixed in this to help him, I'll think twice about jeopardizing his life. He bragged how he nearly killed El. It's a hard thing to talk about. Elvis wouldn't voluntarily have any part of them. So after the others left him, this beast of a human being molested him so forcibly El burst arteries and blood vessels until he was gushing blood all over, even all over Katzman [a relative of producer Sam Katzman]. No wonder El said, when I found him, that he felt like he'd been turned inside out and everything in him was bursting. No one will ever know—I don't think one man in 5 million could have experienced such pain and fear and degradation.

And even while the guy's threatening me, he's making it almost impossible for me to hold back from doing everything possible to have him punished. Yet I know there will be other vengeance. I'm the only one who can witness for El. The only thing we know about the others is that one of them lives—or stayed—in that white house. Anyone who would do what was done to Elvis, is out of his mind. And would do anything. The whole thing is, they were probably high on something which made them very brave and bold and they didn't give a thought for anything after.

They were like vampires—cutting locks of his hair and drinking his blood. Only vampires do such things, and vampires aren't real. I'm just thankful they didn't mess up El's face. He has terrible burns in his armpits and the base of his spine. I saw them when I tried to get him into a robe that awful Sunday. I'll never forget it. I saw Elvis for a minute last night. He had a great deal of pain when he woke up. The doctor said he could expect to have pains similar to a woman's labor pains. They had given him sleeping pills but they weren't doing any good when I was there. He was in a cold sweat and was joking to cover up. Even his composure of keeping distant from everyone had crumpled. So all he could do was try to laugh to make me feel better.

But I saw the sweat and the way he struggled for air and his performance failed to fool me. Then this morning, I saw him for about two minutes before that call came. He said "I can't talk to anyone. Please forgive me but I just can't talk about it." I pressed his hand and left him to himself because he's awful hurt. And if he spoke, I don't think that right now I would have the words to answer him. I did say "Elvis, no matter what, you have two who love you and are with you". He nodded that he understood, but even that nearly brought tears to his eyes, and he closed them and cut himself off again. That's one thing he must be assured of—that we care and don't care about—well—that we understand. Now.

I have to make a terrible decision. What am I to do? I'm half-crushed myself. What can I do to help him? They can't be allowed to get away with it. They just can't, Carmen. They can't.

Marlon

Mid-September 1968

The general public, and even many close associates, did not know the seriousness of Elvis's condition while he was in hospital. Most did not know he had been admitted and believed he was on a well-deserved hiatus. We may never know whether Katzman planned the abduction to occur during a time when Elvis was expected to be out of view.

Sam Katzman

In the following letter, Marlon reports to Carmen a meeting he had with Elvis in the hospital shortly after admission. Again, the medical details may not be accurately described, but the emotions he writes about are honest and raw.

When Marlon refers to Elvis's "uncle," he is indicating Vernon Presley, publicly regarded as Elvis's biological father. Some close friends and relatives of Elvis, however, know that Vernon is not Elvis's father. In a letter to Carmen, Elvis claims that his father was a man named Virgil Presley, a brother of Vernon, which would mean Vernon was Elvis's uncle. It is a long and convoluted story originally revealed in *Letters from Elvis* (page 44.)

Since that book was published, however, I have come to believe that Elvis was telling the truth about Vernon but was not entirely forthcoming in revealing his real father's name, perhaps to protect him. Alternatively, it is possible that Elvis misunderstood or was misled about the identity of his biological father. The identity of Elvis's biological father is still under investigation. Nevertheless, Marlon Brando believed in Elvis's assertion that Vernon was his uncle, and so he consistently describes Vernon as such in his letters to Carmen.

Please guard this very carefully, Dear Carmen,

I guess El's had everything in the book thrown at him. Both kidneys were failing and then there were blood clots lodged close to his heart. They were able to dissolve them, but then this morning his uncle called and told him they had decided to operate this afternoon. They performed surgery on one kidney and took out his appendix and a few other things in order to try to save the ordeal of a kidney transplant, which might fail anyway, and to try to keep the poison from spreading with his reproductive organs.

So far he's doing as well as expected, except for one area: New clots are forming close to his lungs, always a sensitive spot for Elvis. I saw him for a few minutes before they took him, and I had a little talk with him. It was one sided, but I think maybe it's gotten results because for the first time he's fighting hard. Now he needs luck, too. I showed him your card and read the note. I talked to him. He wouldn't let himself respond, he turned his head away from me, and closed his eyes.

Right then I grabbed a hold of his hair and yanked his head around. I guess I was a little stern but sometimes one needs a shock to counteract another shock. I told him "Don't think you're going to get away with turning your back on me!" I said, I knew how he felt, I know all he wants is to die! But I told him that's exactly what his not going to do. Because if he did, certain people will get away with what they've done. I'm not about to see it." The only trouble is, whether they get away with it or if they don't get away with it, Elvis will have to go through more hell, a public hell of the kind that will degrade him to death. It matters how we understand what we think of him. Elvis has to live with himself. And that's a hell of a thing for any man to live with.

It's really worse than such a thing happening to a woman, because its abnormal, and it's hit his sensitivities so long open from old wounds, and it's hit his self-pride. Those hours of torture would be enough to make the average person flip, but for someone of his sensitivity and pride to be made helpless and be so possessed is beyond imagination. And so far they are getting away with it because Sam Katzman swears that both boys were with him fishing up near Arrowhead, and they have two trumped-up, paid-off witnesses. Besides, he said he feels it would break El to have to through court proceedings and his all for getting a couple of strong arm guys and dealing with those bastards the only way they understand.

Then Elvis's uncle said he's afraid Elvis will go after them and kill them. He feels there will be no holding him back once he's on his feet. There's a limit to turning the other cheek. Now where is it going to end? Only in more pain and misery for Elvis. Well, at least he's holding his own right now. I feel he will bounce back, but he will never be the same, and he's going to have to be watched constantly because anything can trigger the deep melancholy in him. I don't think one man in several million could truly understand how he feels. I'm expected to leave next Tuesday and I can't see how I can keep my mind on work.

If there are no more complications, Elvis is expected to go home—and never again to that house—which he loved—by early next week. But after 11 years, the past horror complete with nightmares is still with him. How long will it take to recover from this second horror? A lifetime of horror, or death to stop the nightmares? I'm so afraid and I'm sick from it when I think of those horrors while I sit here.

Marlon

The last paragraph of this letter raises questions. Clearly, Brando fears Elvis may attempt suicide to end his long history of horror and nightmares ("…death to stop the nightmares?"). But to what is he referring when he writes "But after 11 years, the past horror complete with nightmares is still with him"?

Eleven years before this letter was written would have been 1957. The only incident I can find in the letters to Carmen or the historical record is a letter from Elvis to Montez in which he describes a beating he endured in 1957. He gives Carmen the details of resulting facial scars that require makeup to cover. It seems to have left a psychological scar on him as well.

Mid-September 1968

In the following letter to Carmen Montez, Marlon explains how Elvis managed to escape the Katzman gang and call Marlon for help. He also describes more sordid details about the destructive behavior of the gang.

One unresolved mystery regards a reference that Marlon makes to Elvis's blood type. In this letter, he is under the impression that Elvis has a rare blood type. But in my research, I've learned that Elvis's blood type was O Positive, the most common blood type. Somehow, he must have misinterpreted a statement by a medical professional. It is true, for example, that type O Positive blood "is in the highest demand," but not because it is so rare; the reason is that more people have Type O Positive blood, so more transfusions of type O Positive blood are needed overall. Such talk could have been confusing to Marlon, who was in a heightened emotional state at the time.

Dear Carmen:

I'm just sick, Carmen. I don't have the right words. This poor kids' been dragged through the kind of hell you can't even imagine for the last 32 hours. it's unbelievable that any human being could be so sadistic, brutal and fiendish.

Elvis was beaten till his body is mass of welts. But with a professional touch—no broken bones and nothing where it shows, this after he was brutally mass raped by all ten of them—over and over he said, for nine continuous hours, and in-between he was burned with cigarettes and stuck with needles. Then the beating and then they turned his home into a shambles, everything smashed and ripped the drapes, furniture, dishes—all his clothes were pulled from the closets and slashed, paintings slashed.

The white sports car was turned into a total wreck, 2 others in the garage were slashed up inside. Then after the "party" was over, sometime early Sat. morning, the two Katzman boys and their gun boy stayed behind to torment El some more. It ended in a fist fight between the brothers. The one's sole interest was in beating Elvis up, and this was interfering with Sol's pleasure. He wanted Elvis subdued but not unconscious. Also, he didn't want any broken bones or marks on Elvis's face.

They finally raped him again until he began to hemorrhage, then they got scared and left him there, bleeding and semi-conscious. They doubled back after they locked me up, they tied El's hands around each wrist and the other end knotted securely to two brass loops on either side of the fireplace floor. Then they moved the big heavy mahogany dining table to a convenient spot and tied his ankles the same way with his feet apart and the other ends of the leather around two of the table legs. The harder he pulled to free himself the tighter the leather got, and the table was too heavy to move, tied like that with his arms over his head, and his feet spread out. It gave him about a foot and a half of leather cord to pull against.

The sadistic bastards (excuse me) wanted him to have room to struggle without being able to get anywhere. Finally, hours after they left him, he managed to get his hands free. But in that position it is impossible to reach ones feet to untie them even with free hands. Those fiends, Carmen, were so diabolically clever. Finally, Elvis managed to reach the edge of the tablecloth and pulled it off, and with it cane the phone on top of the table. That's when he called me, but he passed out before he could tell me he was at home.

Somehow the phone receiver dropped into place, and the phone was pushed out of his reach. After more time he got one foot worked free and was working on the other one when I got there. I found him wrapped up in only the lace tablecloth, trying to push himself up onto his knees. He was so dazed that at first he didn't seem to realize I was there. He was half out of his head and trying to struggle himself. He was mumbling something, I don't know what, and there was blood all over the white fur rug under him.

When I got him loose, he seemed to realize for the first time I was there. He started to cry without any tears. When he tried to get to his feet, and with that he started to hemorrhage rectally and so I dropped everything and I ran a called this doctor I know who runs a private clinic, and I called for an ambulance because I knew El was hurt inside and I didn't dare more him myself. He's a rare blood type and this caused me even further fear. Only one other person in all of Memphis has the same type as Elvis. He's one in 40,000 persons. So I didn't want him to waste what he's got.

They finally came with the ambulance and got El fixed up so they could move him. The doctor said he would have to make out a police report. I called Chief Ressoner of the L.A. police force and pleaded with him for half an hour by telephone to not let it out, to subject Elvis to the misery of publicity. He finally agreed to keep the report quiet and in a special sealed file, unless the press asked him about it. He said, if they get wind of it, he will have to answer their questions.

He also insisted that either Elvis or myself hire a private detective to make a full report, and an hour later, sure enough there was a detective on the scene. I went through the questioning and he insists on seeing Elvis tonight, sick and dazed as he is. That's why I have to stick around to be with him.

The doctor just told me Elvis is still in emergency and will have to remain here where there is emergency equipment, and also to have X-rays tomorrow. He was in surgery for about an hour, and if he's been crushed or ruptured too badly—the doctor said it looks as though he had been kicked very badly—then it could mean major surgery [as it turned out, major surgery was not required]. So please pray for him that this will not have to be. I'm just thinking how thankful I am that Elvis couldn't get completely loose before I got to him. I'm afraid he would have gone for his gun if he could have made it. I'm personally going to have these guys' scalps for what they did to a good kid like Elvis. If this gets out, Elvis is going to rock this town like nothing that's ever happened before. He can't take that, Carmen. I just hope this detective will give him a break. I'll write more after I talk with Elvis later. Then I can tell you what his state of mind is.

Marlon

Mid-September 1968

Marlon's own abduction, and the torture of his buddy, Elvis, seems to have boiled into a toxic steam that finally blows up. Marlon got into a fierce argument with Elvis's manager, Colonel Tom Parker, who told Marlon that Elvis was more depressed and desperate than Marlon had known and revealed a gruesome detail of the torture that Elvis had not shared with Marlon, probably because Elvis was so humiliated by it.

Colonel Parker confers with Elvis during the 1969 production of *Change of Habit co-starring* Mary Tyler Moore.

In the following letter, Parker suggests that a "citizens committee" of Elvis friends has committed to get revenge and attempts to recruit Marlon, who declines.

This new information and Parker's bloodlust sends Marlon over the edge, and he drives to the Katzman mansion to provoke a confrontation. We don't know what Marlon wants to achieve, but even when he personally identifies Katzman's nephew as a perpetrator, the producer denies that he or his relatives have been involved.

By the end of this letter, Marlon seems to be considering Parker's suggestion of revenge.

Dear Carmen;

I guess Kit's told you by now that I've been in a fight. Sam Katzman and I tangled last night over Elvis. I've got a beautiful black eye, the other one's swollen shut, my nose is a little flatter than usual, and the rest of my face doesn't look so hot either. Of course, a few other people don't look so pretty this morning! Colonel Parker told me something that made me madder than I've ever been in my life and I had to go have it out with that Katzman bas... gentleman!

I called Parker because I had the matter of last weekend on my mind. I told him I didn't think it was right his doing what he did to put Elvis in that hospital. Parker argued that anyone who does some of the things Elvis has done lately is not completely right in the head. He said Elvis threatened to kill himself right there in the hospital. He apparently made the threat directly to Parker.

I told him, "Look, Elvis was desperate to get out." So Parker said, "I'm not blaming Elvis. He's been driven out of his head and he doesn't know what he's doing." Then he went on to say threats against Elvis have come in even to Parker at his home. Elvis doesn't know about this, and Parker went on to say that there is only one way to deal with people like that, and he has gotten together some of Elvis' closest friends to form a citizens committee to "give them back what they've given to Elvis", and he said if I were a friend of Elvis I'd join them and put my argument where it would do the most good. I argued this point, knowing Elvis' feelings on certain things and fearing an all-out war.

I told the Colonel if he hadn't interfered with the police, they might have done something by this time. This infuriated Parker and he countered by telling me something Elvis never told me, and it made me boil over with enough anger to act on my own. Parker said "so you know what they did to that boy last year? And you say they don't deserve to get it back?" I said yes, I knew all about last year. I knew he was attacked and hurt badly, and it was a bad thing. Parker doesn't pull any punches with his speech so I have to quote his retort.

He said "you don't know the half of what that boy went thru. He wouldn't tell you because he went through it because of you." He said, "Do you know how they stuck a red hot poker up his rectum and when he was writhing in agony they tried to have improper intercourse with him?" He said "Do you think I'm going to let those sadists have their satisfaction with him and do nothing about it?" Then he was nearly shouting when he said "you say I'm not thinking of Elvis. I won't stand by and see any human being or an animal hurt like that, let alone Elvis. If I've pushed him it's because his work is all he has and if he's left to sit around and brood he's not going to need friends. He's not going to need anybody but an undertaker."

That went all over me. I became angry like I haven't been since M. King was killed. Maybe even more so. I don't believe Parker would lie about such a thing. I hung up and I went to Sam Katzman's home and I laid it on the line. Of course he denied that his nephew would do such a thing. He called Elvis "queer" and put another word I can't mention in front of the word. He called me a liar, and ended up propositioning me. That's when I hauled off and hit him. I'd have done it before if he weren't such a fat slob. The coward wouldn't fight but he called in a guy who works for him and me and this guy had it out but good. I haven't cooled off much even now, and I'm wondering what the repercussions are going to be.

By damn I feel like pulling someone apart with my bare hands. If they even touch even a hair on Elvis's head again, I'll go after them myself. Because I'm pretty hot now. What they did to him was inhuman. I can't believe such cruelty can exist. He has a letter for you. Elvis, I mean, and I can't let him see me looking like this, so you may get it late. I don't like to make him wait, because I know one little thing can set him off right now and talking to one of us right away could save him from one of his moods. Not that he doesn't have a right. My God, he's suffered cruelly and for no reason.

No wonder he couldn't stand up when I found him. I knew he was in terrible pain but he never said a word how bad it was. That brother of ours has got a lot more guts than I'd have thought. If he were out of his head, he'd have every right to be. Now I've got to do some thinking myself. This can't go any further. I am mixed up in it. Someone even tried to harm him when he was close to death. God knows what I'd do if I were Elvis. Maybe it is up to me, and to others who care, Carmen?

Please advise me. I'm most disturbed. I'll see the picture tonite or tomorrow.

Thanks, Marlon

September 18, 1968

In this letter, Marlon learns from Elvis more details about the brutal acts of torture. Later in the letter, we learn that Elvis has been revealing this information in response to questions by a detective, and Marlon has been allowed to be in the room.

Besides the sadistic tactics used by the gang, Marlon sadly reports the mental state of Elvis in grim terms: "completely exhausted;" "void of any emotion;" "like a robot trained to give facts;" "a complete sealing up of his heart and soul."

Dear Carmen

I've just seen and talked with Elvis. He's coherent and didn't want to want to talk with anyone, but Elvis is not stubborn when someone is trying to help him. He may want to die more than any- thing else he wants right now, but he will not be discourteous on purpose. I know how he feels. I know and understand. Maybe for the first time I fully understand Elvis. We're the only ones who can help now. Maybe sometime later the right girl. But as cooperative as he was I felt his inner turning away. I could feel a door shutting tight and our problems are only beginning. I could feel something very strange and nearly unexplainable. I could feel a part of him dying.

Whatever he does now I can't blame him. Even if he got his gun and shot them all. There were ten of them in all. He said whatever it was they forced him to swallow, made him feel sick at first. Later it seemed to act as a stimulant because his senses became very clear and sharp. One of the guys lived in the motel you described. They went there, Elvis was not noticed amidst all the others in the car. When they changed their minds and were afraid to draw attention so they back tracked. They tied Elvis up, ripped off his shirt and levis, and one of them took his boots. After that he said it was more than nine unending hours of misery. They burned him with their cigarettes, cut some of his hair off in front, and finally one of them came up with what he said was a very large needle, too large for a hypodermic needle. Someone else said it looked like the needles they use in a hospital to take blood samples.

He said they were all drinking and by this time were very drunk. They started taking samples of his blood. Sol Katzman's brother emptied a needle into a glass of whiskey and forced Elvis to swallow the whiskey mixed with his own blood. When the others started using him as a cocktail mixer. When most of them got tired and left, sometime after midnight, Sol let his brother beat Elvis. That belt left bloody gashes all over him. They left him there for the night, drank some more, then went and cut up his clothes and finished the house wrecking job.

In the morning they started in all over again and before they left, kicked him very badly in the stomach with the heel of his boots. By that time, he had started to lose consciousness and doesn't remember who it was. He doesn't seem very clear from that point on. He couldn't talk anymore from here on. He was completely exhausted. Everything he related was void of any emotion—like a robot trained to give facts. That's just how he seems. Words seemed to roll off him. I guess I didn't have the right ones to begin with.

I'm desperately worried for this brother we've adopted. As I left, I happened to notice a television in the corner of the room. After the detective left us, I tried to draw his attention to the TV. I said you would be close to him and you would watch his picture Sunday. And he even had a convenient T.V. so he could watch it, too. Carmen, Elvis didn't even bat an eyelash. I could have said it in Greek. It didn't even bring any "don't try to cheer me up" reaction from him. It brought absolutely nothing, no skepticism, no sarcasm, no appreciation—nothing, nothing. Just a matter of fact telling of—what happened, and then a complete sealing up of his heart and soul and mind as though I didn't exist, as though he didn't exist.

I'm really frightened, Carmen, I'll check and see how he is in the morning before I drop this letter off. I know I won't sleep tonight. Sunday morning. Carmen—I went by to see Elvis. He won't talk to anyone. He doesn't refuse to talk to anyone. He doesn't protest anything. He just looks right through everyone as though we don't exist, me, the nurse, the doctor. It's frightening, we don't seem to be in his world anymore. How can I cope with him? What can I do? I'm at the end of words. I'm so tired myself and I'm so mad and so shocked, and so very, very sorry for Elvis. But that's not enough. Now I need help to help him. I've got to get an hours sleep. Then I'll get this to you while I can still think straight, my head is spinning with a sickening disgust and fear and helplessness. That poor boy.

Marlon

On September 25, a few days after this letter was written, Elvis flies back to Memphis for some additional convalescence. While at Graceland, a good friend of Elvis, Dewey Phillips, dies at the age of forty-two. Phillips was the first radio DJ to play Elvis records on the air. I have often wondered what Elvis must have been thinking about Dewey's untimely passing, which had come so close to Elvis's own brush with death at the hands of the Katzman gang.

Elvis attends Dewey's funeral at the Memphis Funeral Home where services for Elvis's mother, Gladys, had been held ten years earlier.

Dewey Phillips on WHBQ was the first DJ to play Elvis music on the air.

Early October 1968

This Brando letter to Carmen Montez is unique because it shows for the first time in his letters that Marlon has some religious, or at least spiritual, proclivities. Several times, we have seen Marlon ask Carmen to pray for his friend. But in this letter, he confesses that because of recent events he "went to church and really prayed." He writes that he received an answer to his prayers, and this answer was a confirmation for him and Carmen and Kit, the screenwriter, to work even harder on their script for the good of all humanity.

Marlon's words seem genuine and heartfelt, not pandering to his friend, Carmen, an ordained minister in her church. Apparently, he found solace and motivation by going to church. He writes, "I was so discouraged when I went into church, but I came out determined." This is truly a spiritual side of Marlon Brando that may surprise many.

Dear Carmen;

We've got a real fight on our hands, but I'm not going to give in and give up. Elvis doesn't want to do "Chautauqua"—he doesn't want to work anymore—he just doesn't want to do anything anymore. He has to fulfill the contract, unless

M-G-M changes their mind. Against his better judgment, Colonel Parker is trying to make M-G-M angry with Elvis so they will pay him off and get somebody else. I think this is the worst thing Elvis could ever do to himself. I know how he feels. He is numb. He feels empty and he feels he cannot put out and do a good job.

On the contrary, if he will only keep going, forget himself and throw all he can into his work, not only on this one picture, but stand up and demand better material and put all he has into it—until you can get to him—until something brings him to and brings him out of this and he gradually comes alive again—well, this can be his only salvation. He says he can't even feel pain. He feels as though he's under one great big dose on anesthetic, and he's no good for anything.

Now, we can give up and say there's no use doing anything for our project, because Elvis isn't ready to co-operate, or—we can go ahead in faith and put so much into it, work on him, mind and soul as we've never done before. I was so frustrated, Carmen, that I went to church and really prayed. I mean really—not just the repetition of some automatically learned prayers.

The answer I got is that I must work—you must work—and somehow Kit [aka Joi Sommers] must work, harder than ever before—and by harder, I mean with a stronger faith and perseverance and purpose - no matter what Elvis says—and when we do this, our reward will come, and it will come thru him. But no matter what he does, no matter what he says, we have to combine our strength with God's will, and I'm sure that is for all of our good—and we cannot give in. If he won't fight, we've got to do it for him, until he is able to help us fight. Even if it means fighting Elvis. We need him, and only by bringing this need out in the open—by knowing him, by gaining or regaining his confidence, by fighting for him and letting him know you need him and his ability—by making him feel he has something left in him to give, it's the only way he will conquer. And if he goes down, we all go down in one way or another so we also have to be selfish enough to not let him do that to us.

So if you have to be mother and sister, and I brother· and father, and if we have to bring Kit in to provide the missing link—then we've got to do it. I was so discouraged when I went into church, but I came out determined. This may be our own great personal trial and our necessary drive. When you know you've got to do something, you do it.

I'm glad you have an instrument in the script. Without it there would be no tool to work with. It's plain now that this is important, yet it is only the tool or key to other things even more important. There's only one way to get Elvis on his feet now. He has to be needed. He has to do it out of love. Therefore, he must be made to love, to want to give more than to take. No one can give him anything that would replace the emptiness he feels. But while he's alive, there is still in him the capacity to love and to give, and this must now be drawn out of him so that a new purpose can be kindled in his life. There is so much in him that he doesn't know. We see it even if he can't see or feel. So now it's up to us.

I'm anxious to hear about your weekend and Doug Lawrence.

Love to you –

Marlon

October 19, 1968

By the first of October, Elvis has moved to his Palm Springs getaway in Riverside County, California, to recuperate. As we learn from this letter, he is communicating with his friends and showing concern for others. Marlon has been visiting Elvis but ends up staying overnight because he is not feeling well enough to drive back to Los Angeles.

During his stay, Elvis and Marlon talk more deeply than usual about personal matters. Marlon feels, though, that Elvis is still holding back and suspects that his buddy may be more candid in his letters to Carmen. Since we have many of Elvis's letters to Carmen Montez, we know this is true. So is Brando's assumption that the opposite is also true. Based on the evidence in these letters, Elvis was clearly selective about which details he gave to Brando, Carmen Montez and Colonel Parker. Only by reading all the letters to Montez can we get a full picture of the incident.

Dear Carmen

I got sick the other night and had to stay overnight in Riverside [El's place]. I didn't want to stay over because of the talk, for El's sake. But I just couldn't make it back, and I couldn't even get a room of my own because they had a big race on Sun. and everything was full-up. So El had a cot sent up and he slept on it and made me take his big bed. He was so kind and considerate. He put cold towels on my head and made me eat soup and wouldn't let anyone come in the living room of the suite so I wouldn't be disturbed by noise. I don't think he slept very much himself. I woke up at 4 A.M. and he was propped up on one elbow thinking. He didn't want the light on, but once I turned it off he felt like talking. We had a good heart to heart talk. I don't think he opened up as much to me as he has to you, but it is a start. There are some things he possibly wouldn't talk about to a sister as freely as he would to a "big brother."

I guess an experience of the kind he had would leave anyone emotionally disturbed. The girl, his feelings about her, and even his mother are only a part of the whole frustration. He has many fears, many guilty feelings which he should not have. But he thinks they're his alone. He doesn't seem to realize that he's perfectly normal and he reacts in the way any other normal man would react, using common sense and good morals. Unless he opens up and brings these fears out, he will never come to understand he's not different from anyone else.

El likes women and he needs their company. He can't turn off every human emotion just because he lost the girl he loved. He will always love her, she's part of him. But there is life to be lived and he has the capacity to enjoy it if only he'd let himself. In his marriage he has been disappointed but he's learned a few lessons from it and now he has to apply them so he won't make the same mistakes over again. The funny thing about Elvis is, as unhappy as he himself may be, he has a way of making others around him feel like their lives were standing still before he arrived on the scene. Something happens - people begin having fun and acting alive when Elvis is around—on the set, at a party, or just at home—it's always the same way. Elvis brings a certain vitality with him that lights up the whole scene or environment. And it's catching. I think it's one of the factors that has made him as big as he is. Anyway, I'm glad he tried to get some things—if only a very few—off his mind. It made me feel like I'm not wasting my time or imposing myself on him for nothing.

He and I have to get back to working together at least twice a week while he's here. I think Wed. nights and Saturday afternoons. I'm feeling better again. I didn't like the flare-up. The old fever. But I guess it can only be expected—as long as it doesn't stay. Talk to you later.

Love,

Marlon

This last paragraph suggests there have been other communications between Brando and Montez that we don't know about—perhaps missing letters, telephone calls, even face-to-face meetings. This is the first we have heard about Marlon's "flare-ups," which Marlon believes Carmen would appreciate without further explanation. None of our letters indicate that Brando and Elvis are meeting twice each week, apparently so Marlon could coach Elvis in acting technique.

Skeptics who claim these letters are all forgeries have claimed that gaps in logic and ambiguous statements like these are evidence of fraud. I believe that only an extremely clever and ambitious forger would go to the trouble of introducing such real-world letter writing issues. It would be beyond most humans.

October 20, 1968

By the time this letter was written by Marlon, Elvis was back in his Trousdale Estates home, the site of his abduction, though he had once vowed not to go back there. Marlon, who had been a constant companion during convalescence, was about to leave town for several days. Elvis apparently had recovered well enough to reshoot a scene for the movie *Charro!* though he was still plagued by nightmares and some physical weakness. In just a couple of days, Elvis will begin pre-production on the movie being called *Chautauqua*.

I wonder what a collector of celebrity correspondence who owned the following single letter would understand from the text if he or she did not have the context of all the other letters to Carmen Montez. That collector certainly would not understand that the mental and physical symptoms Elvis was experiencing were the result of a traumatic abduction and episode of torture. The collector might conclude that these symptoms were the result of stress or fears. If the collector were also a historian, he or she might put these conclusions into writing, which would introduce yet another strain of incorrect assumptions into the historical record. The canon of Elvis's history would be augmented by more theories accepted because of their alignment with an already flawed historical record.

It does not surprise me that so many Elvis "fundamentalists," those who have spent a large percentage of their time researching and writing about Elvis, are skeptical about letters that expose the cracks in a life story that is already filled with numerous inconsistencies. These letters dismantle many of their core beliefs. I wish, however, that some of them would take the time to study with an open mind a set of letters that, if written about any other famous person, would be declared a breakthrough in scholarly research.

Dear Carmen;

I'll feel a great deal better about leaving if I know Elvis will be able to get in touch with you if need be. He probably won't tell you, but he was a pretty sick boy tonight. I worked half a day and then went to have dinner with Elvis. We ate on the patio because it was warm. While I had a steak, soup and salad, Elvis had half a cup of soup and about two ounces of milk. And I understand that's how he's been eating lately. Elvis said he had a headache, got up and started to run up the 3 or 4 steps into the living room, and with that he fell, flat on his back right through the glass patio door. I ran to him. His head and back were inside the living room and the padded rug saved him from perhaps a concussion, and miraculously there wasn't a scratch on him as far as I could tell. We called a doctor and 2 of his boys helped me get him to the bedroom. He came to after ten minutes and after the doctor looked at him he came out and watched the picture a little later from the couch.

The doctor says he's not eating enough, and Elvis himself said he's been having nightmares, and these things come back to him worse at nighttime. The only sleep he's had in the last three days has been a few minutes now and then in the daytime. And not much then because he's been over at the studio all this week. This morning they shot a retake on "Charro" with Elvis and Lynn Kellogg. They shot it with his back to camera so his beardless face wouldn't show. I don't know if he told you the trouble the Kellogg girl was giving him, but she gave him trouble in the original take - wiggling up to him and things like that—whispering not so nice words in his ear during a love scene—and he was generally uncomfortable. Today was no exception, and in his state of mind, Elvis doesn't need it. All of these little things are building up, Carmen. He's so tired of the whole thing, he's ready to climb walls to get away.

In less than a full year he's had enough to crack an even stronger person. He has a stubbornness about him that has saved him so far. That and a guardian angel. But what when you're not around, and I'm not around. If we don't get him on his feet by Xmas time I'm afraid of what will happen when he goes out on tour. That's going to be rough. Everyday I've been a little afraid for Elvis. I'm surprised he's born up as well as he has. There's a wildness under El's calm composure. Like the rush of water, and once the anesthetic has worn off his nerves, this thing could take him over. Indians have no fear for some of the things we fear. But dishonor is their greatest fear.

El may put on an award-winning show, but underneath he's never been the same since that terrible incident. He didn't want me to tell you about tonight, but I had to. Because he needs help. And that is the only reason I'm breaking confidence. I had the dream again last night. Just as before. Meanwhile nothing has happened with the police. More questions, that's all.

Well, I'll try to write before I leave, but if I don't have the chance, with Harry leaving and Tony coming, I'll be thinking of you and missing everyone. And I hope the next week or two brings about results for you and Elvis and Kit. If my script is instrumental, I'll be happy.

Good luck and my love,

Marlon

October 22, 1968

Marlon issues another Elvis health report to Carmen just as his friend is preparing to shoot *Chautauqua,* a movie with which Sam Katzman is not connected. Filming will continue until December 18, 1968. Considering what Elvis has been through recently, it seems extremely courageous to me—or perhaps foolhardy—to begin another movie project. According to Marlon, he is still having trouble manipulating buttons on his clothing. Nevertheless, while watching Elvis perform in this sub-standard movie, I can't see him physically faltering, but editing may have cut around any issues. He does appear at times, however, to be detached from the whole thing.

Dear Carmen;

Well I've finally been able to sit down and write after all week! I find with El here things have been really hopping. I am taking it easy in one respect however—he's really murdered my love life!

Elvis is going home Sunday. He's up and around but he's woozy and gets dizzy spells and feels unsure of himself. Next Thurs. he's supposed to go in for wardrobe fittings. Fortunately, there isn't too much wardrobe, the only thing is right now he's having trouble just standing up without falling down. The doctor says he's going to have dizzy spells for months to come. Maybe longer. The Colonel had someone scout all of Texas for blood and they finally flew in a pint. But El is still under the line.

The upset over Pris didn't do him any good either. Shocks like that go to his head and bring on the dizziness the same as over exertion physically. The kidney condition seems to be clearing up much better than was expected. And he's now starting to pick things up and buttons with his right hand. By next week, with exercise he should have regained reasonable control of his hands and arms. Of course. he's had aching arms and muscles. But he's yet to complain.

The Karate has kept him in good condition and my putting those wrist bands on him right away helped to strengthen his wrists. He's going to have to wear them most of the time now. Until yesterday he couldn't turn on the water faucet or turn a doorknob. But the wounds are healing very nicely but I still don't trust to leave him all alone. It's his outlook now.

There are wounds deep inside him that have never healed. The Colonel doesn't realize this. I think he's rushing Elvis too much. He doesn't realize his inner needs, and not realizing this he thinks work will cure his ills. Work will keep him going—on this I agree, because Elvis applies himself to it with a real dedication—but—work will not cure him. What will happen when his job is finished, unless this thing eating away at him is cured, or satisfied, or at least tranquilized? The Colonel doesn't know how chronically depressed El is. He's just not in condition to do a picture. He's going to be blacking out all over the set. Yet if I know Elvis, he will put up a front and smile broader than ever to cover up what's really inside him.

They changed the name of his picture "Chautauqua," and what they changed it to nearly brought on a black out spell to Elvis. Hold on—it's now titled "Girls in Trouble and How

They Get That Way!" Elvis said "They've got to be kidding" when Parker told him. He shook his head and said, "You've got to be kidding"—and all I could say was echo "You've got to be kidding." It took some time to convince us both that they weren't and it's for real. Man, that's straight out of "True Confessions" and not at all fitting!

Gandhi, I'm afraid, may not get going at the rate it's going now, until I'm too old and feeble to be able to read the lines, let alone play the part. [The movie *Gandhi* was filmed fourteen years later in 1982 without Brando.] All I can say is this is a crazy business. I do think you should work on Parker, however distasteful, and there isn't much time now. Time has always been your worst enemy.

I do feel a good feeling about Lawrence, so see what you can get him to do now. It will be made known as of Mon. that El's in town, and if he has to do the things Parker wants him to do, he might as well have one more meeting, one that will be profitable for him. I feel it has to come about this March, through anyone or any way it can happen. I'll keep you posted for Elvis and I may write you later for him.

Marlon

P.S. I just found out what all the yelling was about between the Colonel and Elvis the other day. Elvis wanted to hire back 4 or 5 of the guys for bodyguards and the Colonel said the Federal Government will no longer allow Elvis to salary so many guys. It seems there was a check-up on his tax report and the Colonel was very upset. Elvis can do this on his farm or on a large estate such as Graceland because they are listed as hired hands there but living in a small 2-bedroom house the government is questioning it. They put a limit and said he can have 2 bodyguards and 1 secretary in the house. Elvis was pretty mad about it. Today he said he was going to go and hire himself 6 pretty female karate experts to share his home, and maybe the government wouldn't question that arrangement. It seems no matter what he does someone is there to squash it. So, I guess he has given up the idea of getting Tom [Yokohama] back, will keep Alan Fortas as bodyguard and Joe Esposito as secretary. Joe is someone you would get along with very well.

Marlon's postscript claimed that Colonel Parker had told Elvis that the federal government had authority to control the number of bodyguards he could hire to protect Elvis. This is patently ridiculous unless Parker was using these employees in a tax dodge. More likely, if Parker said this to Elvis, it was a lie to explain why he was trying to limit expenses.

Early January 1969

I don't have any Marlon letters to Carmen that were written between the previous letter and this one, perhaps because Marlon was preoccupied with promotional activities for the upcoming release of his most recent movie, *Candy*, which satirizes pornographic stories through the adventures of its naive heroine. Besides Marlon Brando, the film contains an odd assortment of movie stars and celebrities of the period including Richard Burton, Walter Matthau, Ringo Starr, James Coburn, John Astin, Charles Aznavour and Sugar Ray Robinson.

This letter conveys to Carmen Montez a tale of betrayal that profoundly affected Elvis for years to come. The traitors were Elvis's wife Priscilla and a trusted member of his extended family. Marlon was both an eyewitness and a participant in the story he tells Carmen.

Dear Carmen;

Well, I think El's really had it. There's murder in his heart right now. Last night I called him when he got home and I asked if I could drop by about 9. He said yes. I took a short cut through the back, past the bedroom windows. I saw a lite in

El's room and I was going to knock on the door when I saw Priscilla was there. So I went around to the living room and Elvis' cousin Patsy let me in. She knocked on Elvis' door and presently Elvis came out and we talked for a while, I gave him a lesson and we went to the kitchen and had a glass of milk. I tell you this, because in doing these things about an hour and a half passed.

Patsy was with us and made some sandwiches and then I left as I came in by the short cut. Oh—meanwhile I had told Elvis I'd seen Pris. I was surprised. He said lamely "Well, you know how I feel, but it's Christmas and all, and you know how it is." He had as much as said she had gotten her hooks in him even though he didn't really want it. I figured after all he's been through he might be better for having a woman around and I let it drop. Anyway, as I left, Elvis' room was dark, but there was a lite on in the guest room where his cousin and her husband live. As I passed I couldn't help seeing Pris and GeeGee [Marvin "GeeGee" Gambill, Jr., husband of Elvis's double first cousin Patsy Presley.] and they weren't playing checkers. Lights on and all. They didn't expect anyone to be out there. I said a little prayer Elvis wouldn't know.

She had obviously been with him less than an hour and a half before I got home and I didn't have my keys. I had to go back. I went around the front, we found my keys and then over my protests Elvis had to go to his room to get a book I'd loaned him on theory (acting). When Pris wasn't there he went looking for her. He finally knocked on his cousin's room and the door was locked. He knew she was there. He shouted for them to open up. Patsy came running. Elvis broke the door, and Pris was right in the bed with his cousin's husband. I'm telling you, Carmen, I thought Elvis would kill them both. Patsy went white. Elvis got out the luggage and threw it and everything in the drawers out the door, then went after Patsy's husband and half killed him outside, then he picked up Pris and threw her out, finally picked up Patsy yelling that two more could play the game, and he locked Patsy and himself in his room.

I finally banged on the door until Patsy got it open. I was afraid he'd take his frustration out on her. But she said he had just grabbed her and shaking all over he had started to cry, and the only thing that was keeping her from going to pieces was trying to keep Elvis in one piece. Now tonight he's gone off the deep end in another way. He's made a nice public date with Connie Stevens to go to the fights. And that isn't like Elvis. He's done it on purpose, and I don't like it, Carmen. Whatever happens, please, please don't let him get involved with a woman like Connie Stevens. You know what's going to happen after tonight? By morning it will be all over Hollywood that the two were out together. That gal's nothing but a tramp and all he needs is Eddie Fisher on his neck. Elvis is doing this on purpose. He has a little vengeance in him and I can't blame him, but it isn't worth destroying his name over Priscilla. This is something Elvis holds high. Now is when he needs a good woman, not that kind. Please help him get hold of himself. I'm greatly concerned.

Marlon

Elvis had dated Connie Stevens back in 1961. Singer/actress Stevens is perhaps best known for her role as "Cricket," the perky photographer/nightclub singer in the TV series *Hawaii Five-0* starring Jack Lord.

Brando's "concern" for Elvis increasingly seems more like a kind of fetish. I wonder if the actor's continued concern about so many aspects of Elvis's life might have caused Elvis to start feeling smothered by his friend. Over time, Elvis may have started to withdraw from the relationship, causing Brando pain and anger, which eventually led the actor to lash out at his old friend years later.

Singer/actress Connie Stevens.

Mid-January 1969

Donna Douglas, the singer/actress mentioned in this letter from Marlon, is best known for her character role as Elly May Clampett on the TV series *The Beverly Hillbillies.* Elvis met her playing the role of Frankie in his 1966 movie *Frankie and Johnny*.

Singer/actress Donna Douglas.

Dear Carmen;

I'm really getting worried over Elvis. I think he's flipped or something. He's just not acting like himself, Carmen. The night he took Connie Stevens to the fights I waited for him to come home. I called and called and finally he answered. He told me to come over. I no sooner got there that Stevens walked in wearing Elvis' pajamas. Elvis blushed—actually blushed to high heaven and said "It's not what you think." Well, I didn't say what I thought but I left.

The next night I got home about 3 a.m. myself. Who was getting into her car in front of El's place but Donna Douglas. The next day I was shooting some retakes (Fri.) and I bumped into her in the commissary I asked her if it was her I'd seen leaving Elvis's house the night before. Tactless maybe, but to the point. She was mad as a wet hen at Elvis. She said "that guy's crazy. He got me up there at midnight just to hold his hand. I told him to call the babysitters agency!" whereupon some other chick joined in with "If it's Elvis you're talking about I'll hold his hand any day!" I don't know what he's trying to prove, but he's surely not himself. I wouldn't say a word if he was normally like that, but he isn't, and a man can't change overnight. He's in need of a lot of straightening out, Carmen, and you and I are the only ones who can help him. Besides—he doesn't even go for blondes! I think the kid's lost his head. All I know that Douglas girl was real put out. And she's really some good-looking girl, too.

I feel like El's kind of avoided me, except when he gave me the letter. Then he was evasive. Said he was going to church and was in a hurry. So please see what you can do. I think that wife of his has got him going in circles so he can't see straight. El's a good kid only he's not a kid anymore. But he is young and vital, and I think he's just now beginning to find himself as a man and he's got to come to terms between himself and some of his inbred ideas. Ideas such as his are fine to an extent, but let's face, Elvis may be spiritual and a good guy, etc., but he's still flesh and blood and his blood isn't the watered down kind. So he's being untrue to himself by refusing to look himself in the eye. God made him just the way he is and there's nothing wrong with him just the way he is. But he's only frustrating himself by not facing up to his own strength.

I've seen a lot of strength come out in Elvis in the last few months since his ordeal, Carmen. He's got what it takes all around. But he's ashamed of himself on one hand, and yet when he lets go he forgets it and he becomes himself, as you saw when he was performing. He becomes a different person when he lets himself go. He responds to people and this satisfies him and they respond to him. I'm praying this tour will bring him back. Anyone with that much to give has to give it or it will devour him. Elvis has to give—as a performer, as a man, as a friend. They're all one and the same. Elvis is part lamb, and part tiger. And the two parts of him will not call a truce. If he could only see himself and know that both have their place. I can tell you what I think, but it's very difficult to make him see it.

Anyway, if a man ever needed help its Elvis. So do your best.

My love,

Marlon

February 1969

This letter expresses Marlon's concerns that Elvis "fears he's a latent homosexual." If so, the brutal sexual abuse Elvis endured at the hands of Sam Katzman's thugs may have been awakened that fear. It is interesting, however, that Marlon addresses this issue with Carmen Montez.

It is widely known today that Marlon's many sex partners over his lifetime included men. Numerous Brando biographies have presented his bisexuality. In a 1976 interview, Brando said, "Homosexuality is now so much in fashion it no longer makes news. Like many men, I, too, have had homosexual experiences, and I am not ashamed. I have never paid much attention to what people think about me." Among the celebrity partners he has been linked to are Wally Cox, Quincy Jones, Burt Lancaster, Laurence Olivier, John Gielgud, Leonard Bernstein, Noel Coward, Tyrone Power, Montgomery Clift, James Dean and Rock Hudson. To balance the ledger, he had numerous female sex partners and was married three times.

Was Marlon Brando captivated by Elvis's stunning good looks? Of course he was, but this letter, in which Marlon "sometimes thinks he [Elvis] fears that he's a latent homosexual," suggests to me that these two buddies never openly discussed the topic much less acted upon any physical attraction Marlon may have felt; either that or these Brando letters contain an element of gaslighting.

Dear Carmen;

Well, it looks like Elvis really doesn't feel like talking to anyone. I know he's there shut up in the house, and I know he got the note I left him, but he hasn't responded. I didn't think Pris would get to him this time. I mean get under his skin. Especially if she made him so mad in Memphis. I just don't know what is wrong with that little girl. She's been hurting him so much. She could have been the one to get him over all the hurts of the past. The thing that happened to him so long ago was something that couldn't help leaving scars on him. He's just begun to find himself as a man. And a patient, understanding wife could have done wonders. Now Elvis, partly out of morality, and partly out of fear, won't turn to another woman, and he seems to fear other men. So he's being churned up inside until he fears himself. I sometimes think he fears that he's a latent homosexual.

Sometimes I'm afraid I'm losing my mind—times like when I see Indians running around! But there's usually a logical explanation. Even if he had that in him doesn't mean he has to go that route, when it's obvious he doesn't want to. If he only had a good wife to help him. It's what he needs so badly. Well, I just wish he would come and talk to me. Sometimes it's almost as if he's afraid of me. He needs someone, Carmen. The more he searches for companionship, the more he meets the wrong people, and his confusion deepens. Well, maybe he will come out of it and talk to me before he leaves again. If he doesn't, I'm going to feel like I let him down.

Until later, Marlon

March 19, 1969

Marlon tells Carmen Montez in this letter that he is concerned about his friend Harry Belafonte's physical condition. As a small boy, Belafonte had been taken from his home in the West Indies to the University of Miami for serious eye surgery. In early 1958 he had eye surgery again. Now, in 1969, Harry is facing the need for an additional procedure.

It has always seemed odd to me that Marlon begins this epistle with his concern for a friend before mentioning the more sensational news that one of Elvis's rapists had just been found murdered. This tidbit, of course, presents a potential dilemma for Elvis, whom Marlon fears could become a suspect in the crime.

Like many other letters by Brando and the other letter writers, this one rambles a bit, one of those human characteristics of spontaneous personal correspondence that is not intended to be well-organized and polished. In these letters, the more important information is sometimes buried, and the opening is casual—even banal—by comparison. Not until the second paragraph does the reader learn that one of the brutal members of the Katzman gang has been murdered.

Dear Carmen;

I've had several upsets over the weekend. Harry [Belafonte], of course, upset me a great deal. His doctor will be here from New York Tues. morning, and if it's possible to operate, it will probably be done on Wed. Harry is in a near state of panic because there are so many things unfinished and so many things no one else can do. Not only the play he's producing on Broadway, his one-night tour, and a television appearance in an acting capacity, but also the political and the fundraising, and the secretive undercover work. In itself, what he had before, but each time it is more frightening because the chance of repair is lesser. He's been going at such a great pace without a moment to collect his thoughts. He's under great mental and physical strain and he needs to stop and do some of the things he needs for himself. He's had very little time for any of his loved ones, and that isn't good. He made such a point about wanting to write and talk over some things with you.

Besides Harry, I told Kit to tell you about the phone calls I had at the studio Friday morning. I told the police, and Tom Parker. Sunday morning, Sol Katzman's brother was found at the bottom of a canyon near Culver City. His head was bashed in and his neck broken. Need I say he was very dead. The thing that frightens me most is Tom Parker's words: "I've had it with that no-good pair. They're not going to hurt anybody else anymore." Between us —what do you think about this? I don't want any blame to fall on Elvis. Some of Katzman's own bunch could have done it, but Elvis could be accused of planning it. He has a motive. I know he didn't— but others don't know him as we do.

I'm not so sure about somebody else though. I hate to even harbor such a thought, and I wish you could shed some light on the matter for my own peace of mind. I don't know whom to tell about these things any longer. Elvis took the news with a straight face. No sign of any kind of emotion. I'm afraid for Elvis. He's existing like he's shot full of Novocain. I don't know how he will be able to manage this picture. He can't walk through it in a trance.

This thing might blow wide open now. Until now both those boys had paid alibis. The police found a lock of hair in this guy's wallet. Dyed hair. Only thing is, Elvis has washed the dye out of his hair, so it doesn't match. If it had matched this would have linked Katzman to Elvis' beating. I'll tell you the truth—I think both Katzman and Parker—each for their own reasons have paid to hush things up. Katzman doesn't want the scandal and Parker doesn't want Elvis linked with that bunch in case people start to believe he was one of them. And that would hurt at the box office. Also, he's afraid Elvis will break if it came to going over all of that in public.

Parker is genuinely fond of Elvis, but he's also coldly calculating. He once rigged it up for the police to come and arrest Elvis on stage in Houston for an "indecent act". He knew Elvis would never go for it, so he didn't tell him. Just arranged it and let them cart Elvis down to the station. He was never booked, of course, but all the photographers and reporters just happened to be on hand to greet him at the police station. He has a way of doing what he thinks is best for Elvis. Elvis dislikes this, yet the Colonel has done a great deal for Elvis. And he does have an iron-bound contract. There seems to be so much interference, but I'll bet anything that nothing will happen, and someday, sometime, if it's another dozen years, Elvis will again be jeopardized. And I don't like his having to live in fear. I think that's worse than anything. I really wish you knew the outcome.

Right now, I only hope you can soon get close to Elvis, because these weeks of brooding will eventually come to an end in disaster, unless he finds the way and the reason to pick up his life. And just as Kit needs a new factor in her life, Elvis needs one in his. They each need something to take place in their lives, outside of their own doing, before it is up to them to mold their futures. I know now that it does depend upon the proper combination, and on all of us being really together—in a new concept.

Hope you're feeling better. I'll give your message to Elvis, and I hope you can get him to talk to you. If he'd only pour it all out it would be far better than this silence and keeping it in himself. It's as if words are no longer important to him. He hasn't left the house, Carmen, hasn't even spoken to the studio. The Colonel's bluffing it all, guaranteeing Elvis will be there for wardrobe fittings next week. I thought he could talk to you and to me, if no one else. We'll see what you can do. And I'll give any message you want to Harry. I'll see him first tonight, and then stop by Elvis' on the way home.

Harry's in the hospital in Santa Monica.

For now, my love and good wishes.

Marlon

March 20, 1969

Marlon relates to Carmen a humorous episode in which Elvis rebuffs the obvious advances of a gorgeous actress, Lynn Kellogg, during the filming of *Charro!* the previous year. Marlon's detailed telling of the story seems to reflect his delight in Elvis's determination to ignore the distractions and show off his best acting chops to the great actor Marlon Brando, who was allowed to observe the filming.

Elvis with members of the *Charro!* film crew.

Dear Carmen;

I wanted to get this to you from Elvis bright and early, but I gave a party last night, and I'm dead today! Several people wanted to give me a birthday party, so instead I invited them and some other people I've neglected of late to a pre-birthday party, because I feel by my birthday I will want to spend it a little more quietly with the friends closest to me. Also, Harry will be in on the 5th, and of course the 4th is the 1st anniversary of M. King's death, and I really don't think I'd be in the mood for a big party too. Easter week I'm hoping to have Chris [Marlon's son Christian Brando] with me for 2 weeks. He's such a big boy now, Carmen. You wouldn't know him. He's quite a boy despite everything.

I was terribly upset over what happened to Elvis Fri. [This refers to breaking news that the Katzman relative had been found murdered.] He was rushed into this picture [*Change of Habit*]. Parker, fully knowing his condition, pushed him, and when he was unable to fulfill the requirements as expected, he was rushed off to a hospital, not for the care he really needs so badly, but to answer questions and be prodded at by that kind of doctor. It was a bad shock for him. It's caused him to run away for the weekend, alone, when he should have someone with him. He's likely to keel over at the wheel the same as he did at the studio. The boy's anemic and weak, not insane. But he's in the perfect frame of mind to be driven that way. El said not to worry, he would be all right, and he'd be back Mon., but nevertheless, I have worried. Can't help it. This boy shouldn't be driving. God go with him.

I called the residing Dr. in charge of the Bel-Air hospital. He told me Elvis was suffering from exhaustion, coupled with a deep and intense depression. Then I later talked with Parker at my party after Elvis left. He came to talk to me. He said,

"Elvis is like my own boy (I doubt it) but lately he's been way out, and if he's sick he should have treatment." Then he re-assured me he would never expose Elvis to "that kind of publicity," [the sexual abuse] and whatever happened [such as retaliation] it would "be kept very quiet." I wish I could talk to El before Mon. morning. I want to caution him to try to hold on and go easy because I know him well enough to know he can't take this. He needs patience and love.

Oh, how I wish he had a girl to really love him and look out for him. Now is when he needs it. He's starved for love like a man dying of thirst in a desert. Well, I'm anxious to see what our boy can do in "Charro." I hope his first dramatic attempt doesn't come off too badly. El got along very well with Ina Balin [Elvis's co-star in *Charro!*] but he didn't go for that other girl, Lynn Kellogg (who played the role of Marcie in *Charro!*]. This one's got quite a figure, but she played up to all the fellas around Elvis. I was there when they shot the dance hall scene, and the girl took her red scarf or whatever you call it and draped it around Joe Esposito, Elvis' friend and secretary, and just played up to Joe.

I remember one other day I met Elvis on the Goldwyn lot and we went to his dressing room for sandwiches. The trailer was parked so its back window was almost even with the dressing room building's windows, and because of the limited space it was almost back to back with Lynn Kellogg's dressing room. I happened to glance out of the window while El was making the sandwiches, and there was the Kellogg girl going around without a thing on. I made a remark, but Elvis kept on with the sandwiches without looking up or batting an eye. He just sat down with his back to the window and explained that his venetian blind was stuck. (Convenient, I thought!)

Later I went on the set with him. He was most eager to impress me that day, to show me what he had learned from me. It was a scene where El was laying close to the Kellogg girl and she was running one hand thru his hair. There was brief dialogue and the camera was shooting from about their shoulders up, and there was scenery and props in front of them. Well, El kept fluffing his lines. I could see his face was flushed and he was getting mad. He even looked embarrassed and uneasy. I knew he wanted to be good that day for my benefit. One time he put his head down, saying his lines thru clenched teeth. The director yelled "cut" for about the 7th time.

Finally, on about the 8th or 9th take, El made it dialogue-wise, but he was blushing furiously. The director stopped him again, asked what was wrong, but Elvis only shook his head and started again. They made it finally but he looked very disappointed, so I didn't ask him about it just then. That evening at home I asked him what was wrong. He said that inasmuch as Miss Kellogg was one of his leading ladies, he had to be a gentleman. But he added that it's very hard to concentrate on lines while someone is running a finger up and down your spine. Elvis is very easily distracted, and I can just imagine the distractions he was subjected to.

It's a pity that when he tries the most, the forces always seem to work against him. He has a very dramatic arrangement of the theme song. There's so much feeling running thru his voice if they only didn't hold this feeling back in the picture. Next week will tell, I guess. The sneak reviews weren't so good. But it may be that people aren't ready to accept a bearded Presley. I'll try to get to see it Fri. or Sat., and I'm curious and anxious to see the results of my labors, as well as El's efforts, and your opinion.

Till then, love,

Marlon

Lynn Kellogg, who appeared with Elvis in *Charro!* (1969)

April 6, 1969

On Easter, 1969, Marlon penned this letter to Carmen about the movie business, especially the recent reviews of Elvis's western, *Charro!*, which were generally uncomplimentary. This segues into a short essay about the script that Carmen, Joi Sommers ("Kit") and Marlon are attempting to move forward into a development deal. In the end, Marlon stresses how important it is for Carmen to meet personally with Elvis about the project, underscoring again that he understands the value Carmen places on pursuing a career in the film industry.

Dear Carmen;

I want to wish you a truly happy Easter and I hope we all will have peace and contentment—you and Kit, Harry, Elvis and myself. I think we've all striven toward this goal and I kind of feel we deserve it. I guess we pretty much agreed on El's picture. I said I'd go into it a little more, so I'll take a few minutes now. I thought it was too slow at times, perhaps it was so to me because I couldn't stand some of those other characters. The reviews said the camera work was bad. However, I think Elvis got some good camera work, far better than he's had in many a picture.

I feel more and more sorry for Elvis, though, the more I read the reviews. It seems the public is just unable to accept him as anything except the strolling troubadour. They said "Stay Away Joe" was dirty and how could Elvis do it. Yet "Joe" could hardly stand up to the average picture going around today. It was ridiculously mild compared to films like "Three in the Attic", "Sister George", "The Sergeant", that Paul Newman picture just out, etc. Then "Live a Little" wasn't accepted too heartily, "Speedway" was run of the mill, and now "Charro" is not El's cup of tea they say. It kind of upsets me because – well, "Joe" was a trial—a try at getting El away from the same old musical. But for all its flaws, it showed him as a man. "Speedway" and "Live A little" are two he should never have done, and "Charro" again leaves much to be desired as a film masterpiece but that is not El's fault. However, he seems to be getting the blame for the entire fall down—for the direction, for the editing, for the works.

I do think the professional reviews should give credit where it's due, but they seem dead set against El somehow. He's going to have to be Gable and Cooper and John Wayne all rolled into one before they'll acknowledge that he's even competent. I thought he was very intense, strong without brutality and had a certain confidence that was becoming because it came from earnest endeavor and not cockiness. I still say, with or without our help (and I hope it's "with"), Elvis is going to surprise everyone as an actor. For the simple reason, Carmen, that he applies himself and everything he does, he does well. Whether it's cars or horses or guns or karate. He strums a mean guitar, though he's very modest about it, he'd surprise you on the banjos, and he has a long ignored talent for lyric writing and arranging though he doesn't read music. He's shy about water skiing and dancing in public, but he has the rhythm for being a fine dancer, and anyone with the coordination he has for roller skating can make it with the skies.

El thinks he's a dull homebody, but he's greatly talented and everyday he surprises me with something new. El's eager to learn and I'm hoping so hard you'll be able to get to him before going thru Parker. Even if you fail where the script is concerned—and I do feel Elvis will like it, even if some of the others won't—even if you strike out on that score, Carmen, you still have two other very important goals where Elvis is directly concerned: Elvis himself, his need of counsel, and what you can do to help he and Kit get together. El needs someone like Kit and if he doesn't soon meet a girl like her it's eventually going to be some other girl. And frankly there are a lot of lookers around, but few I know I would like for Elvis. Kit is just right, and furthermore, he is just right for her. And let's face it—her life is at a standstill simply because she needs the right person just as he does. And if something doesn't happen there, she, too, will probably go on looking, and eventually find someone else—equally wrong, and he in for more heartbreak.

So if it's only for this, I hope you succeed. I hope there will be an opening for you, and for Kit in El's life, regardless of the script. So if you do meet and find the angle is not working out as planned, do all you can to find a way to further your other causes. That's why it's so much more important for you to get directly to Elvis. I feel the script was inspired—it was meant as a tool to open a door of far greater importance. If it serves this purpose it will be a success even if it goes no further than fostering friendship and love between all 3 of you.

Good luck and have a blessed Easter,

Marlon

May 23, 1969

As if learning that Elvis had been abducted and tortured is not enough brutality, in this letter from Marlon we learn that singer Tom Jones, a good friend of Elvis and Marlon and a confidante of Carmen Montez, has also been abducted and tortured along with his manager, Gordon Mills, who died in 1986.

Gordon Mills (left) with his client Tom Jones.

Admittedly, the information reported by Brando is second-hand, but Tom Jones also reports the incident to Carmen as explained in *Letters from Elvis* (pages 229-234.) If some of the details in the following letter are incorrect because of misunderstanding or failures of memory, I have confidence that the incident occurred generally as Brando augmented by Jones's own first-hand description attests. This account, purportedly describing another attack by the same gang that molested Elvis, portrays abduction followed by torture.

Dear Carmen;

I wanted to get this letter to you earlier than this, but I had a few personal problems of my own, so please forgive me because I know it is important. I talked to Tom [singer Tom Jones] a while ago and he's still shaken and he's hurt but if not for a miracle it could have been worse for him. As it was, Gordon Mills [manager of Tom JonesO got the worst of it. They had been over to Caesar's Palace talking over the contract for Tom there next year, and then they decided to walk over to the Flamingo, Tom's old haunt. As they were walking through the casino on their way out a crowd gathered, as usual, only this time, after Tom signed the autographs, etc., a couple of men tagged after him. He and Gordon went out the side entrance, and two more guys were waiting for them there. These two pulled guns on them and marched Tom and Gordon back to their car, the other two men joining them across the street, Tom and Gordon were waiting their chance for the men to drop their guard so they could fight them, but the 4 of them had guns, so the chance never came.

Tom said they drove he and Gordon to an abandoned mine out in the desert, where two more men were waiting. They were in what used to be some sort of an office above part of the mine structure, (gold mine in the old prospecting days) and once there, Tom and Gordon were tied with their hands over their heads to some kind of support beam. Tom said the gang was high on what he termed a "speed drug". They kicked him and Gordon, ripped their clothes off, leaving Tom in just his famous red undershorts, they tried to make him take some drugs and when he would not, one of them cut him with a knife on the abdomen, thigh and upper arm.

He said he was afraid they were going to try to attack him the way they did Elvis, and he started praying the roof would fall in. He put all his strength into trying to pull loose, that suddenly the floor fell in, and Tom and the beam and all fell through where no one could reach him. When they couldn't get their hands on him any longer, or figure how to get him out, they turned their full wrath on his manager and beat him up very badly. They left him half dead, but he came to around daybreak and managed to get his hands free and when he found Tom hadn't broken his neck or anything else, miraculously, Gordon managed to get one of the fallen beams or planks down in the hole, which Tom said was like being at the bottom of a well, and Tom finally managed to get out that way. Which isn't easy to climb out of something even with a plank as a ladder when your hands are tied and you're dragging around part of the building to trip you up.

Anyway, once up, Gordon and he together got him loose and Tom, in Gordon's shirt and his red briefs, made his way about 5 or 6 miles to the highway. The police are checking, but, like always, I'll bet it will be dropped after the proper person pays off! Gordon is hospitalized and Tom can't work tonight, may just make it for his closing. He says he's sore and bruised and scratched all over, and though the cuts are superficial, they are painful when he puts on clothes, and he wouldn't be able to get into clothing tonight for sure. Besides, he's stiff and tired, and he got a gash on the left side of his back, and after being crouched like that all night in a position like he was in, his back and neck and everything is acting up, and no one knows what the outcome will be yet.

He's lucky, yet very unfortunate, all at one time. Tom said to keep him in your prayers and he will talk to me tomorrow and Sat. and keep us posted. If I were there now I could help. It would happen right after I left. So I'll let you know whatever happens. And I'm only glad it wasn't any worse, although I'm afraid it would have been more of what Elvis went through if they'd have had their way.

Elvis will be back in Las Vegas tonight. He couldn't get a plane this afternoon or he'd be there now. So I hope he will be careful. He wants Tom to come in here with him over the weekend, but Tom said no, he has to be in Vegas. He will be without Gordon for at least two weeks.

Well, I've got to run, but I will keep you posted.

Marlon

June 9, 1969

This letter from Marlon has nothing to do with Elvis, but I include it because it is a small but sweet correspondence between two close friends. After the preceding darkness, I felt the need to give the reader some light.

Carmelita

Happy Birthday Dear Carmelita—

Because of my illness I have been unable to leave the house to get you a birthday present as I wanted to do. But I have given Kitten the money for you both to go out to lunch on your birthday or whatever day will be convenient for you. Also, I brought back from Japan this small token which I'm giving you. It is just a small "something" to remind you of me. And I think it will go well in your apartment. Forgive me, Carmelita, but my thoughts and best wishes are there with you. Can't write much right now. My arms are affected and bother me at the present time.

Happy Birthday and lots of love,

Marlon

P.S.:

I enclosed a small silk print which I also brought back with me from the orient with intentions to mount someday. I thought you might like to add it to your collection of oriental articles for your future "tea house." The work is all by hand by very fine and patient laborers.

July 25, 1969

In late July, Elvis was about to depart for Vegas for a series of shows. Someone—we don't know who—organized an elaborate going-away party that featured a band and close friend Tom Jones as a featured entertainer. Even Elvis sang a few songs. But then something shocking occurred.

Dear Carmen:

It's been such a trying day for all of us. I feel very sorry for poor Tom [singer Tom Jones]. Elvis wanted to write but he was so upset, and he has his hands full. It strikes me such a senseless thing. It started out as a surprise-going-away send-off-party for Elvis. It turned out to be a surprise all right! There were 50 people, more or less on the patio and nobody even knows for sure what happened.

The musicians were having a jam session, their girls and wives were there, plus a few crashers and some people from the hotel in Vegas. Elvis decided to try out a couple of his show numbers, then he introduced Tom and they did a routine, then they start to outdo each other. It was very hot, and Elvis finally laughed and said he was going to save his strength for Vegas and went and sat down at a table to

Tom's right. There were people sitting and standing all over in a circle. I was in front of Tom but a little to his left.

Tom tried to get away, but everyone kept applauding and crying for more. They let Elvis sit down probably because he was the host, but they wanted more and more from Tom. He wasn't singing at the time, just standing there doing what he does. He suddenly bent his head low, almost doubling up but no one thought anything of it. There hadn't been a sound. They apparently used a silencer. He was so taken by surprise he just stood there for several seconds with his head low like that then I heard him say very quietly "Will somebody please help me. I've been shot." He said it so quietly that only those standing closest to him had heard above the music. I rushed there and one of Elvis' bodyguards and some other fellow, but Elvis didn't seem aware of what had happened until we took hold of Tom and were helping him to the nearest chair. We didn't even know where he'd been shot.

Then El got through the crowd and by the time Tom had taken those few steps he had started to bleed. You know the 1st thing he said to Elvis? "There goes another pair of pants"!

Someone called a doctor and Gordon Mills [manager of Tom Jones]. Gordon Mills called the police before he even got there. They wouldn't let anyone leave after they arrived, but about 1/3 of the guest, mostly the women, had already left. They questioned the crowd, then questioned me and Elvis, and finally got to Tom after the doctor had finished with him. Meanwhile we had taken him into Elvis' room. In fact he walked once the shock wore off. You can imagine how he felt, up there performing and the next minute a bullet in his leg. t struck the inside of his left thigh high up near the groin.

At first when he started to bleed Elvis thought it had hit him in the groin but then we found it had passed clean through the inner side of the thigh from the front to back, and the bullet was later found lodged in the cement of the patio.

Tom doesn't have very much fat on him but fortunately it struck a more fatty spot and the doctor said it had injured only one major muscle, and it had passed through clean so there was no surgery needed and he can stay where he is and just have the doctor come in and redress it. Also, in his favor, he had all kinds of shots in preparation for this trip, so there shouldn't be any serious complications. It's going to interfere with his plans though since the doctor said to keep off the leg for at least 3 days, maybe a week. Exercise later, but not the kind he does for a couple of weeks. Probably not until his next taping and then he should take it easy. Of course, we know he won't.

Elvis didn't want him to go home alone, but Elvis is leaving Sun. night and he really doesn't want to go and leave Tom with a bad leg and no one around him. Mills will be leaving Wed. He has to lineup the T.V. show in London. Tom was going to fly up to Vegas Wed. and join Elvis, then leave there Fri. or Sat. I don't know what they'll work out now.

Tonight, Elvis is having 2 of his bodyguards sleep out on the patio. He's worried, I know, that someone will come back. He called 2 extra fellas, 2 inside and 2 outside for tonight at least, maybe until he leaves. Elvis and Tom were going riding tomorrow before Elvis left. They're both excellent horsemen but this fixed that for sure.

I guess you heard about Tom being Knighted this fall. It's going to really burn the Col. because his title is of his own doing!

What else can happen?

Marlon

July 31, 1969

During the day of July 31, 1969, Elvis performed a full-dress rehearsal—two complete run-throughs of the show with full orchestral accompaniment. He was really charged up.

That evening, the Sweet Inspirations began the opening-night show while Elvis suffered a panic attack until he finally stepped out on stage at ten-fifteen. With almost no fanfare, he appeared from the side, hesitated briefly, and then rocked the house with an all-out rendition of "Blue Suede Shoes." The invitation-only event attracted celebrities such as Cary Grant, Pat Boone, Carol Channing, Fats Domino and Marlon Brando. Elvis was radiating energy like a light ball throughout the showroom.

Elvis and Cary Grant chat after a 1970 show at the International.

Shortly after the show, Marlon wrote this letter to Carmen Montez.

I'm anxious to see the reviews. They couldn't be bad.

Dear Carmen;

I'll tell you later what Elvis gave them—everything. Elvis was really great tonight. He was so alive and vital. He came on like a house afire. I must say he put everything he has into it. He shook and shimmied and shouted and cried. I caught real tears in his eyes at two places. One time was when he sang the song "Memories." This is the song that would be just great for our story's theme. You might suggest it to anyone interested if you agree. Because I really like it, and it brings out a great deal of emotion in Elvis. He was like electricity throughout, throwing off sparks.

I also caught a few barbs thrown in very slyly in Priscilla's direction. Personal things no one else would notice. The strain of "Are You Lonesome Tonight", which he quickly turned into a joke, but Pris got the meaning behind it. Elvis dreams of a better life. But I'm afraid it's a dream of heaven.

His closing song expresses his dream, this dream which is so much a part of him. It expressed it beautifully. Yet I'll bet very few understood it. His hair was its natural color. And he looked great in the leather suit. Although he said it was like being in a sauna bath under the hot lights. He was wearing his silver and turquoise good luck rings. Elvis loves rings.

There was an informal party—a gathering really, of Elvis 'close friends afterwards. Sandwiches and coffee and champagne for those who wanted it. And Elvis looked really excited about the show. He had a glow about him I haven't seen since that awful experience. Even before, I don't think I ever saw it. And it made me happy.

I was sitting with his cousin Patsy watching Elvis talking with some people, and Patsy remarked how she envied Elvis. I asked her why. She said "because he's too pretty for a man!" She said she spent all day at the beauty parlor, and Elvis has all that hair and just combs it. He had a youngness in his face tonight that seemed to erase the tired, brooding look he's had for so long. In fact, lately he's been looking downright strained. Oh, how I pray, Carmen, that that look will fade, and with it the feelings behind it. I'm so hoping his fears and doubts will be replaced by hope.

And I've so much hoped he could know you, I mean really, and that he and Kit could find each other, because I know they'd turn each other on, and she so needs someone like Elvis—not only reliable, but unsophisticated and open and honest. Someone simple and outgoing and in need of love. I've been so afraid he'd built a wall around his heart like the he's had to build around his life. Elvis isn't the kind of person for walls. He hates walls just as much as he needs them. He loves people, only they don't all love him.

Anyway, he was great, dynamic and strangely he seemed very much alive tonight. Tonight, I said something to him about how commercial Xmas has become. The old usual remark cliché. He said to me "Christmas is within yourself. You have to make it. It isn't made with tinsel and holly. You have to make it yourself, from the inside out." It made me feel good when he said that. I not only knew he was right, but I knew he was thinking again. Thinking with his heart. And that's a good sign. This boy's been hurt more than most people could ever comprehend in a lifetime of unhappiness. He's felt so degraded for so long, that I was really and greatly concerned.

Now that he seems to have come alive again, and seems to feel things again, I hope sincerely he doesn't get another blow before he can get his balance. He's like someone who's come out of Novocain, and he would feel any new pain very sharply. So keep your fingers crossed and hope miss Prissy doesn't go around cutting pieces out of him this Christmas. No matter what Elvis says she still has the power to hurt him, and he's so afraid of being shamed in front of her by what happened. I have a weird warming feeling.

Just pray he can stay happy for a little while. I'll write more later on.

Marlon

Elvis captivated the audience in Vegas on July 31, 1969.

Early August 1969

Like a good beat reporter, when he is back in Los Angeles, Marlon fills in Carmen Montez on more news following the stunningly successful opening night performance by Elvis.

Dear Carmen;

I just want you to know that Elvis did exceedingly well. We may have to worry about him in many ways but as a performer is not one of them. I feel he's got more now than he's ever had. His trials have given him a quality that is indelibly stamped in his voice, his gestures, his inner force. Even since last Jan. he has come forth—whether it was being so close to death, or whether it is in part Tom's influence - but I could see it in his work, even since the T.V. show.

Now if he can hold on consistently, and I think he can, he's got it made to do anything Parker will let him do. I hope he's as good when you see him. I only hope they don't change here and there until it takes away from him. I advised him to stick to his guns, and you know, for once I think he will. I'd have given a lot to see him and Tom together, but I felt Harry needed us here. He's really the one I'm concerned about. It's not only his eyes, but where he used to be so calm I sense a great turmoil in him.

Opening night went smoother in many ways than the previous 3 opening nights that I can recall within the last 6 years. No one got out of line, and Harry was feeling reasonably well. There were a great many technical faults, and he was quite uneasy for a while. I think this is what Kit felt and could not define. Harry is usually so at ease even under very trying conditions, but for some reason he couldn't conceal his unrest and tension from those who know him well. I think he really expected some trouble, and I hope it never comes. I could feel his distraction from his performance and several people I know felt it with annoyance.

Also, Linda [Melinda Rose Woodward, wife of Tom Jones, whose real name is Thomas John Woodward] is still in town. What do you think of Tom's wife sneaking quietly back to town, and bringing their son Mark with her, after Tom escorted them back home? I came in early when I heard he was having trouble with his leg. I didn't want him going back to the airport by cab. So I met him, picked up the letter for you, and drove him back! Gordon Mills met him at the doctor's office and would have had the Newman's chauffeur [actor Paul Newman's chauffer] drive Tom to the airport, but again that involved another party knowing about it. The Dr. told him to stay off the leg absolutely for a week. Exercise is good once it heals but it won't have a chance to heal until he stays quiet. He's not suppossed to move about any more than he has to get from one room to another, so I hope he listens!

His deal for the Century Plaza all depends on the way his leg is by next weekend. He didn't want Mills to know it was giving him trouble because he wants to do the Plaza, but the doctor gave him a prescription for what I know to be a very strong pain killer. I know because I went and got it filled to save him from getting mobbed in the pharmacy, and

I've studied up on drugs and chemistry. He'd cut that leg off before he'd admit it was giving him trouble. It's not just the spot that was injured, something like that creates havoc with so many other muscles and nerves that react in sympathy.

Well, I'm going to deliver this and then try to get some rest myself. It's impossible to rest in Vegas, especially around Presley. Elvis wanted to write to you and send a letter with me, but no one gave him a moment's peace. So, he said to tell you he sends his love, and he was very enthusiastic over an offer he had to go to London this winter. They offered him 10,000,000 pounds which is two million and forty thousand American dollars, but I can tell you right now, Elvis' enthusiasm will be short lived because Parker will never allow Elvis to go to London when Tom is there if it's at all within his power to stop him.

Elvis also said to tell you his film finally had its Memphis preview, and is due for a public release within one to two weeks. Also, Priscilla's on his neck and in his hair. Now is a good time—by Monday—to recheck with people like Doug Lawrence who were there, because a great many people promised to come back, and if anyone you know should be there the week you are there, it would be nice if you knew it and could look them up. Otherwise you'll get up there and come back only to discover 10 people you and Elvis each know were there and you missed each other. He did me proud. I'm very satisfied.

Now to deliver these letters and get some sleep before Mon. morning. Until later—I'll be interested on your views about Harry, also—

Marlon

August 9, 1969

For a long time, Marlon has been in love with Kit (aka Joi Sommers) but refused to admit it because his buddy, Harry Belafonte, was more openly smitten by the young screenwriter and friend of Carmen Montez. But Harry knew he was too old for Kit, so he had fostered a more paternal view of their relationship. This letter is Marlon's painful confession to Carmen of the rage he felt when his friend Tom Jones, unaware of Marlon's deep feelings for Kit, seemingly steals her away. For the first time, these two close friends come to blows over a woman.

For years, Marlon has been writing about his desire for Kit to hook up with Elvis because he needed someone other than Priscilla in his life. I believe this was insincere and Marlon subconsciously knew that Elvis would never fall in love with Kit, which would allow her to continue a relationship with Marlon.

We learn in this letter a secret about Kit that Marlon hopes will be an obstacle in her relationship with Tom. We also learn that Tom does not know Kit's real name. In fact, for the duration of their relationship, Tom will never know the true identity of Kit and so assigns her the Welsh nickname *Lwli* (pronounced 'looly'), meaning Baby.

Dear Carmen;

I am at this moment so mad with both Kit and Tom Jones that I could in turn ring each of their necks with great pleasure! Here I am trying to help work things out for her to get to Elvis and she takes off with Tom Jones! I'm so mad I think sparks are coming out of my ears!

It all started when Kit was at my place tonight and Tom called. He was taping some numbers and had obviously written an answer to your earlier letter and he said he had forgotten to come by before he got to the studio and he was skeptical about carrying it with him and changing clothes, etc. So I said I'd drive out and pick it up before he started the actual taping because I knew this involved several changes of clothing and it's very dangerous to have to transfer anything personal such as that. I had already suggested to Kit that we take a ride, so it was not out of my way.

I had to park a block and a half from the studio; I left Kit in the car and went and got in to Tom and got the letter, and then he said there was still time to go out front if I wanted to before they let in the ticket holders. So I ran back to the car and got Kit, and at that moment she was skeptical because she was wearing that sensational, if skimpy red pants outfit Harry had bought her. It's quite something if you haven't seen it. Anyway, we got in from the back and got front row seats, and Tom did a couple of production numbers with dancers and sets, and then something happened about the costumes or scenery or something and after 2 numbers they decided to finish another time.

Angry or not, I mean everything I've ever said about Tom, and more. He felt the audience was being cheated, so after they finished shooting he asked if they would like him to sing a couple of songs for them on his own time. He wound up doing 4. During the first he spotted Kit and got a look on his face. I must say at this time he didn't seem to realize she was with me, and I hadn't mentioned I'd brought anyone. On the 2nd number he came over and kissed her. Kit acted startled, Tom grinned and walked away, but a minute later he came back for more. Finally, he came back and kissed her a 3rd time and before he pulled away I saw he'd whispered something close to her ear. I asked her what he'd said and she said he said to come back stage after he had finished. I said okay. I was all for her making a good impression. So I took her back and we waited while he took his usual shower or whatever. But the scene backstage by this time had changed from what it was earlier. When Tom finally came out what seemed like a hundred kids swarmed around. I waited awhile but it was impossible to get anywhere near him.

Finally, he did hear me call his name, looked up and spotted me, and his eyes went right to Kit. He signaled to wait but I soon saw it was hopeless, so I called his name again and when I caught his eye I motioned we were leaving and I called that I'd see him at home later. He looked disappointed. I spent the next 4 minutes catching his overflow and signing autographs for them. I introduced Kit as a writer and she was even asked for an autograph.

I was glad to get out of the crush and when we got out Kit noticed one of her gold shoes was coming apart, and since it was quite bright and very public I said I'd go and get the car and she should wait there. Well, that's the last I saw of her last night! When I came back she was nowhere in sight. I thought maybe she went back inside, and I asked the usher and he informed me the girl in the red outfit had gone with Mr. Jones when he came out and had gotten into a red chauffeured Cadillac with him. Some woman standing there also confirmed it, said he'd taken her arm and they'd gotten into the Cadillac.

I exclaimed in surprise "Why would she do that?" and the smart chic came back with "you're kiddin'?" I couldn't believe it, Carmen. All the years I've known Kit she's never gone off and left me—and with a strange man! I still don't believe it. So I went to her place and waited for a while. No Kit. I called her; I called Tom's home 3 times. The last time was about 1 a.m. and his wife was irritated, said no, he hadn't come home. So I called Elvis long distance and asked him where would Tom go, including the Sands, if he wasn't at home. Elvis said his manager was staying at the Beverly Hills hotel, had a bungalow there, and he was out of town and said Tom could use it if he should want to, in Mills' absence. I thought it was worth a try when it got toward 2 a.m. and I couldn't find Kit. I called the Beverly Hills, and after I told them who I was, there was a short conference and the night manager took the phone and told me Mr. Jones had come in about 11:30 but he left orders not to be disturbed, and all phone calls to be held until 1 o'clock the following afternoon.

Now I was starting to get mad, so I went over. I saw a light in the back from what appeared to be the bathroom. But nobody answered. There's a patio on one side, the rooms are sort of combined living room -bedroom with a slight divide, and the patio opening off the living room side. But there was a high brick wall. I waited until about—oh between 4 and 5 a.m. The light finally went out completely and I banged on the door to wake the dead. That so and so wouldn't open up or even answer. I finally went home and kept calling Kit. Then at 8:30 I went back, I banged and called, and finally after all that he opened up. He was looking around uncertainly and I asked sarcastically if he'd lost anyone. He said it seemed so.

I check the bath and the patio. He was alone but I observed 2 flat glasses of champagne on the night table beside his 2 rings, and Tom was wrapped like a mummy in a sheet. I asked him where she was and he said smartly "I ate her for breakfast!" Then he said "what's all this about? She isn't your girl." I said no, and he said she told him she wasn't my girl, and then I noticed he didn't know her name and he was trying to find out. He finally admitted she wouldn't tell him her name and right about then I spotted a note on the bureau in Kit's handwriting, and when I picked it up her antique gold pendant with the 2 ruby hearts fell out of the paper. She wrote that she knew they'd meet again another time when things would be different, and until that time she wanted him to keep the pendant from her Welsh grandmother so he would know he would always remain a part of her.

How can he be "part of her?" Somehow I saw red and he reached out and snatched the pendant from my hand and said flatly "It was given to me, was it not?" And he stood there with a grin on his face, and the next thing I knew I wanted to wipe that grin off, so I let go with a punch on the jaw that threw back his head. But he still stood there wrapped in the sheet and grinning. He wouldn't fight me.

He said and repeated: "What did I do?' and I got out before I let him have a good punch in the nose. I guess I'm so mad because I had Kit all picked out in my mind for Elvis. She and Elvis are right for each other. All she needs right now is a man with not only a wife but a mistress besides. I wanted her to make a good impression on Tom, but she didn't have to go to bed with him. I'd like to knock their heads together!

One thing if he doesn't know her name or where to find her, he sure isn't going to know from me! Wait until I catch up with Kit! Aside from a little Welsh blood what do those two have in common? I greatly admire Tom, even if I shall rearrange his nose somewhat, but I'm very, very mad with him. And she should have her head examined. Please tell her I said so.

Marlon

August 20, 1969

Marlon's longing for Kit and disappointment with Tom Jones continues in this letter to Carmen Montez. I haven't been able to locate the photograph of Tom's family that Marlon describes in such detail. In his identification of the people in it, however, we learn that the actress Joanne Woodward (wife of actor Paul Newman) is a cousin of Tom, whose real name is Thomas John Woodward.

A brief reference to "Jim" signifies a young man named Jim Mathews who was Kit's lover before she met Harry Belafonte and Marlon Brando. We learned from Harry's letters in *Letters from Elvis* (pages 163-169) that Jim was a half-brother of Harry Belafonte, thus he had been the original access point to Harry and his celebrity friends. Jim had fathered Kit's son but turned out to be an unreliable partner, which had caused Kit to suffer greatly. Harry and Marlon had stepped in to support Kit and her baby.

By the end of this letter, Marlon has softened his attitude and become more philosophical about the twists of fate. He still wants to protect Kit from harm but agrees, for the time being, to stop trying to manipulate her life.

Dear Carmen;

Well, I don't know, somehow I don't feel that this is going to blow over. I feel impending tragedy ahead, perhaps even for Tom. Mark my words, he grabbed too hard, and he's not about to let go. At first, I thought he would, and that irritated me but I felt it was better that way. Now I feel he'd do it all over again. It was all too quick, Carmen, and she doesn't know him. He spotted her from stage, and came and kissed her, came back for more, then kidnapped her like he was Valentino and threw her in bed with him, ignoring me and grinning like the cat in Alice in Wonderland when he was caught.

Meanwhile Kit was having more troubles with that Jim, and then along came Jones; warm and sexy and Welsh. I wouldn't say so much if she had known him longer. It's just that I don't want to see her go from frying pan to fire. And by his attitude I'm sure he has ideas for an encore. I just think there are times when Tom comes on too strong. I want to see Kit settle down and I'm afraid she never will while he's in the picture. I care very much about Kit. Tom's a big boy—I sympathize for his problems, but he can take care of himself. If he's not finding what he wants at home there are plenty of other women flinging themselves at him. He has a wide choice and most of them would give their right arm for some attention from him and they wouldn't be lonesome afterwards.

Kit needs someone to be with her and give her all the things she's never had. She will never try to find anyone with Tom Jones in the background. The only kind of woman for Tom the way things are, is the kind who won't hang on. Either that or get rid of that wife of his. Two people living under the same roof does not constitute a marriage.

Movita [Maria Luisa "Movita" Castaneda, Brando's second wife] had wanted us to go back together again, but I see we are still as far apart as we were before in our thinking.

She never wanted to make a home for us either. Two people have to work at it. One alone can't do it no matter how hard they might want it. One person said to me after seeing Tom at the Greek Theatre "Tom Jones isn't an evening's entertainment. He's an experience." I only wish Kit would put it down to experience and let it go at that. Anyway—he knows my stand and she knows too. So that's that.

I'm looking right now at the picture of Tom on page 20 of the magazine about Tom and Elvis, the picture of Tom and his family. That's his slightly pregnant sister in the foreground on the right. Her husband, Tom said, is the one in the top left corner. That's his mother behind him with the leopard bag, and her sister to her right, and their mother between the two women with her arm on Tom's shoulder. Wouldn't that be the woman by whom he is related to Kit? I notice in the photograph she bears a striking resemblance to Kit's mother from the photos I've seen of Kit's mother. In back of her on top is Tom's father, and his mother, the one with the Jewish in her next to him, and Tom's youngest uncle beside her. I think that's Tom's grandfather on the other side of his father, and another uncle beside him. One of those uncles must be Joanne's [Joanne Woodward's] father, and another the father of the man Tom's wife is crazy for. I don't know who the others are to the left, they don't look like they belong to the same family. They may be in-laws.

I like the looks of Tom's parents, especially his Dad. Thomas Sr. looks very proud of Tom. I must say, though, those pants are surely tight. He could never get an English shilling into the pockets of those pants. I was just listening to his record like the last one he gave you. He does a great job on it. After listening to it a couple of times one of the songs grew on me that I hadn't particularly noticed before. "Untrue, Unfaithful," etc. I'm not sure if that's the right title, but somehow I like his manner of delivery. Makes me think of Priscilla somehow! I think he ought to dedicate it to her.

Carmen, that girl [Priscilla Presley] looks so hard lately. I wish she would just get out of El's life because people are really beginning to talk about her now. They are beginning to see through her beauty and pretense now and see her for what she is. And she's really embarrassing Elvis. Well, I can't have life the way I'd have it. I just want those I love to be happy. If Tom is just satisfying his male ego where Kit's concerned, she could be hurt again. And it's too much, there has to be a balance somewhere. One can take a little hurt if there is also a little sunshine. And if he's serious—then it can only be Mary all over again, and unhappiness for both of them.

Elvis on the other hand is going to surprise everybody one of these days and say he's had enough of Pris and the whole business. I wish Kit would concentrate on getting to Elvis before she blows that again. He's far more substantial in the long run, and while I know Tom isn't happy in his personal life (he couldn't humanly be happy) he still can take care of himself better, where Elvis needs a woman's touch. Tom can be happy in the company of other men, and in his work and with his family.

But Elvis has no one he can trust—not even a trustworthy manager. Neither is he happy in his work. Tom can only go up right now. Elvis could easily go down, especially with Parker standing behind him shoving. I have a real fear for Elvis if something or someone doesn't come along to help him soon. Tom has done wonders for him. I've helped him, and so have you.

If having a friend like Tom, a true friend he knows he can depend on, has helped Elvis so much, think how much more the right woman could do for his life. And while this need exists, this person to fill the void, why shouldn't it be someone not only able to fill the void but someone who could also be helped by Elvis' friendship and understanding? Kit's got to be practical for once, and certainly Elvis isn't that hard to take. I wonder if Nancy finally gave up on him! Haven't heard any more from her.

Well, it's Kit's life, so I'm not going to interfere anymore. I just wish her well and I wish things were different for Tom. We'll see.

I better get some sleep now. Thanks for the letter.

Marlon

P.S.: Talked to Tony [unidentified acquaintance] and he said to say hello. His skin condition appears to be improved. He's hoping for good news when he goes to see his doctor next week.

Late September 1969

This is a fascinating letter in which Marlon reports to Carmen the results of a chemical analysis of some Sucaryl that he had taken from Elvis's kitchen. For some time, because of Elvis's erratic behavior and mood changes, Marlon had suspected that someone in the household may have been drugging his friend. Marlon originally had suspected GeeGee Gambill of seeking revenge on Elvis because of GeeGee's fling with Priscilla and subsequent banishment by "the Boss."

The letter begins in a way that indicates Marlon had previously mentioned his plan to Carmen to have some kitchen items analyzed. We also learn that somehow the bottle of Sucaryl had found its way to Kit, who had ingested a small amount and become very ill. How she obtained this Sucaryl remains a mystery, but I speculate that Kit had visited Elvis's home for some reason of which Marlon was unaware. Certainly, a meeting of Elvis and Kit could have been engineered by Carmen, who was Kit's manager as well as Elvis's secret confidante.

We also learn in this letter about "Elvis's past record of several suicide attempts," information not previously known by the public.

Dear Carmen:

Well, there was enough acid in that Sucaryl to kill an army battalion! I asked the chemist if it could have been a revenge thing to burn someone's vocal cords. He said it certainly would burn the vocal cords and everything else it touched in one normal teaspoon. It was a dose not to injure, but to kill. So it wasn't Gigi [a misspelling of "GeeGee," the nickname of Marvin Gambill, Jr., Elvis's valet and chauffer] or anyone with revenge in mind. It was meant to finish what it started. Elvis used it at one time at Parker's suggestion, some years ago when he had put on weight. What saved him was that Elvis doesn't drink coffee hardly at all, and he isn't one for cereals. He's a steak and eggs and milk man for breakfast, and there's really very little one adds sugar to except in cooking. And he's lost so much weight anyway, he's tried to put on and not lose anymore.

I'm sure sorry about Kit but I'm glad no more harm was done. The chemist said it was a "slow acid", one that wouldn't show signs of working until the coffee or whatever had been drunk and probably the cup washed and put away. Then it would cause quick hemorrhaging, probably without change of getting help. An autopsy would detect it but with Elvis' past record of several suicide attempts, everyone would assume he'd finally made it.

I took it to a private investigator and found the only prominent fingerprints are mine and Kit's (the size indicating a woman, and in the last several days). Before that it was handled by many persons (probably in the store) and therefore smudged. I haven't said anything to Elvis yet because I have to bring in for Kit. It probably would only upset Elvis and do no real good. I did tell Tom however and he was really upset. I told him about Kit—not by name—but that the bottle had gotten to her. He said "oh, my God! Make sure you get her to a doctor to be sure everything is alright!"

I promised, but my doctor is out of town till Monday. So, since she seems all right, if not great, I'll take her then. Cause I promised Tom and he was greatly concerned for her as well as for Elvis. Meanwhile if anything comes up and Kit feels really bad, I'll have to take her to this doctor whose treated Elvis and Tom. But I'd rather not unless it's an emergency. It's partly my fault and I have to put my own mind at ease. Just wanted you to know about it. I guess there's no sense making Elvis nervous when it's all over. More of this kind of thing and he will really have a nervous breakdown.

Marlon

P.S. I just had an interesting afternoon! Nancy Sinatra tracked Elvis down to my place. How I'll never know, but as a detective she was determined to get her man! That girl's really quite a handful to handle. Elvis was sitting up in bed reading. I heard some commotion about ten minutes later and when I went in (only to make sure El was all right) she had backed him into the shower, had gotten his pajamas off somehow and there was water all over everything, and steam. She'd turned the hot water on Elvis and he was yelling to get out, then she changed it to cold, and he was still yelling and she was wet and her hair dripping and I was embarrassed, and just then I was saved by the doorbell.

One of Daddy Sinatra's aides was looking for Nancy. She said I had to get her out or he'd kill her or her father would, and I said it was lucky I didn't. But her car had been spotted and Nancy left with damp hair and wet shoes and the look on her face was as frantic as the look on El's face, except he was blushing from head to toe. How that boy gets himself into things is as bad as Kit getting into trouble! Never a dull moment. All El had to say is, "After this I can face anything!"

Late September 1969

Marlon covers a host of topics in this letter, including Colonel Tom Parker's financial crisis, his own savage review of *The Trouble with Girls*—Elvis's next-to-last acting performance—and a complaint about the white suit that Elvis wore in the *'68 Comeback Special.*

Since the previous letter to Carmen, Marlon seems to have discovered that Kit had met Elvis at his home. This is made clear when Marlon writes: "I even think the fates let Kit stumble onto Elvis because she had to break that resentment she had developed for him." The reason for Kit's prior resentment of Elvis is not explained in any of the letters in my possession.

Dear Carmen;

I've been more than a little upset over Elvis, Carmen. For one thing he's in such a daze and his physical state was greatly weakened. He wasn't able until today to take solid food. I had my maid cooking soup all week over at the other house. Finally, he had a steak with me today, and since he's never fully built up his blood since Jan. this has done nothing to give him strength.

Then I saw the picture [*The Trouble with Girls*] last night. It wasn't only that the picture was bad (and bad is the understatement of the year) but more than that there was so much pain in Elvis' eyes that just looking at him revived all those days when we kept constant vigil over him. The picture was made between his attacks and finished less than 3 weeks before his nearly successful suicide attempt. Just looking at him you can see what he was going through, the sunken checks, sleepless, pained eyes, and tightly drawn mouth. It was just that frame of mind, so openly obvious, that drove him to what he did only a few weeks later. Elvis didn't care about anything, and for once he couldn't conceal it. He even walked out on Peter Tewksbury [director of *The Trouble with Girls*] and went home one time, if you recall. Something he's never done in his career.

I won't dwell on the picture. It isn't worth the time or the paper. But it was Elvis that left me with hurt, knowing firsthand, and now seeing all over the deep hurt that was put in him, and is still there, in fact. Buried by sincere attempts to overcome, yet nevertheless still there. We both lived that difficult time with him and the subsequent attempt on his life. I saw that look in his eyes, and the tight drawn expression of his face for many weeks. And then when we were beginning to overcome it - this. If Elvis were to break, neither Tom nor I would blame him. I really think Parker and Priscilla are together trying to break him.

Tom's been at work and I should let him tell you himself what he's found out—but in brief, Parker is in trouble financially, because he went into a business venture and he misrepresented the product, and now he stands to lose most of what he has. He needs quick money—by that I mean within the next 6 months. He can't wait for Elvis to earn it for him anymore. He needs it now. Sure, as Kit says Elvis can earn money for him, but that will be through the years. He's in a pinch now. He can't wait. So he has to settle for less now. He probably figures after he gets control of most of Elvis' money, then after a while, if he hasn't killed Elvis by then, he can get him out of the cage and put him back to work by virtue of his name and the loyalty of his fans. Elvis may fade somewhat by then, but he can still earn. It's unbelievably dirty but that's what he's up to.

You alone, really, hold the ace that can win the game. Because he doesn't know you know what cards he holds. But you do know what he's up to and what kind of game he's playing. You do have material that could put Elvis back on his feet. That look in his eyes is the look I wrote about. It wasn't all makeup as Kit supposed. [Kit had criticized Elvis's makeup in *The Trouble with Girls*.] You know, I even think the fates let Kit stumble onto Elvis because she had to break that resentment she had developed for him.

Now that is out of the way, and with your knowledge of Parker, the script as a weapon, and his promise of a meeting as an opener, all you have to do is push his promise through and I think by then you'll know what the next stop will be. And somehow, in some way that is also the turning point for Kit. Whether thru Elvis directly, or through associating forces, I don't know. But I feel she will know—you will both know your own direction at that time. I hope for El's sake it's soon. His uncle [Vernon Presley, popularly considered to be Elvis's father] and cousin Gene will be here I believe on Sun. to take him home and stay with him awhile. I hope that is the right move. Only Parker will find out one way or another where he's been.

Also, Nancy Sinatra's called me, looking for Elvis. She seemed really worried, but he said no, not to let her know where he is because he's not very anxious to see her. I'm surprised Parker has not tried to contact me, but he has not tried to reach either Tom or me. I'd better count my blessings while I may! Anyway, my concern goes on for Elvis. He's still a very tortured man, he doesn't sleep like he should at night;

when he does, he tosses and talks in his sleep. His eyes are gradually clearing. For a while they had a foggy stare, now that is leaving, but beneath the fog is still a deep hurt.

Elvis' eyes take on a brightness when he's hurt. They shine and look almost wet, and they seem to pierce right through you. That look is there right now replacing the fogginess, and even his face is thin and gaunt. Underneath it all he still knew to come home, knew he would be safe with me and near you, and Tom, too. So there still is hope as long as he still retains that defense.

I'm so tired, Carmen, trying to move, trying to keep movers out of this house for El's sake, and trying to remain here when Tom isn't here. So forgive me if I sign off.

Until I hear from you,

Marlon

I still think the right woman would make Elvis get rid of Pris. And this is what he needs—both the right woman's influence and to get rid of Miss Prissy. Tom Jones may be more exciting, but Elvis would be very loving and considerate and understanding, and he wears well, he's loyal and could make an appreciative woman very happy.

I don't think it was so much makeup that was at fault. I didn't notice makeup on Elvis except that the hair was overly black. Rather, he was extremely pale at the time, and his paler contrasted sharply with his dark brows and lashes. His eyelashes are black, and thick as his hair, and while the white suit [worn in the *The Trouble with Girls*] looked good, they should have put something on him with more color. Blue, too, is a cool color, and combined with the white suit and the pale skin, it drained him of warmth. Red instead of blue would have added a glow to his face. But that of course would have been too much to ask from that production.

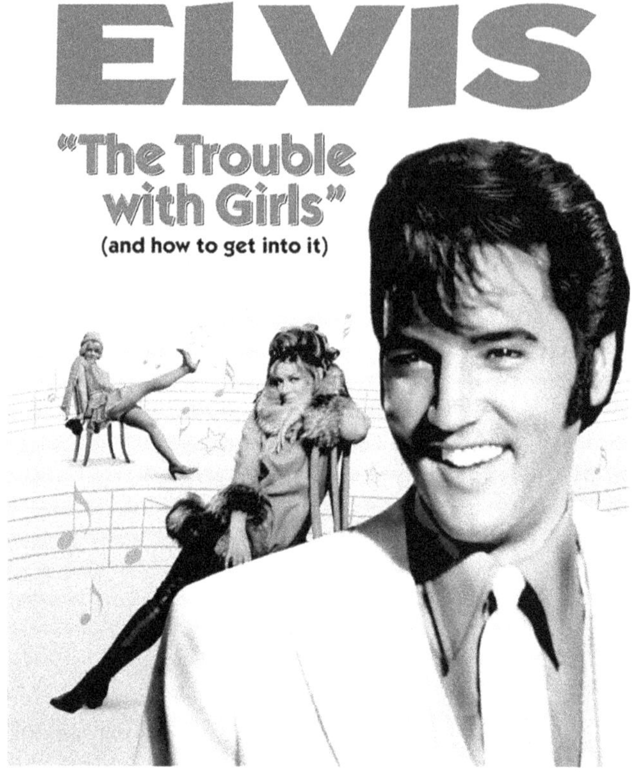

Elvis in the white suit that Brando despised.

October 1969

The following Brando letter doesn't supply background information that explains its opening, but Elvis had recently returned from a vacation in Hawaii, a trip almost entirely funded by the International Hotel in Las Vegas. On October 12, Elvis returned to Los Angeles with plans to continue the holiday in Europe. Colonel Parker, however, canceled the European trip arguing that European fans would be insulted if Elvis were to travel there as a tourist before performing in England or on the continent. A short holiday in the Bahamas was scheduled to begin October 22. While in Hawaii, Elvis spent time with his close friend Tom Jones.

Tom Jones and Elvis in Hawaii, October 1969.

As Brando's next letter explains, Elvis was in a funk when he returned and needing some additional comforting, so Brando called him. Marlon discovered the cause of Elvis's angst—a problem with Priscilla, who was temporarily living separately because of the disagreeable situation. Brando explains the situation to Carmen in a disjointed fashion, then urges an intervention for the coming weekend, probably because Elvis was scheduled for the Bahamas holiday soon after that.

Dear Carmen:

Well I no sooner got Elvis home and settled in his place, than I had Kit to worry about. She had herself so upset over that script that she was sick, so I brought her up here where it's at least cooler (it must be about 140 degrees in her place), and then she was almost blacking out on me from getting all excited and upset.

Just about that time Elvis called me and I blew my top with him. And he didn't do anything. Now I'm sure he must be convinced I had another woman here the minute my wife left. I asked him if he was feeling any better and he said except when he moved his head too sharply, then he got dizzy still. And therefore would I drive him to see Priscilla Saturday nite because he wants to make her go back to her family instead of stay there alone.

That's when I jumped at him. I said "Look, I've got another one just like you blacking out over here. Only this one's female! I'm going to pick her up and bring her over and all you'll have to do is move over because I'm going to throw her down right in that bed with you and you can be sick together or cry on each other's shoulders, make love or sink or swim, or whatever the hell you please!" And I hung up. Poor Guy. He must have wondered what he did. I guess indirectly I was irritated with him because I still think he's a fool even seeing that woman.

It's almost masochistic, like he's asking to be hurt. I don't think I could sleep with a wife pregnant with somebody else's child while I was her husband. Elvis has so much pride, why does he throw it away on someone who doesn't appreciate or care? Forgiveness is fine, so far. At least he's had it out with Nancy. I don't know what she did. but he's terribly angry, far angrier than he was the night of his accident. He says he doesn't want her anywhere around him, including on a movie set. He was livid, too, for someone as easy going as he is.

We've got to do some more talking this weekend—all of us—you too, even if it's only on paper. We've got to get a few ideas going here because I have a bad feeling for that kid. Try to concentrate hard and see if you can come up with something like the time something can happen, or the place, or what to watch out for. The war of nerves is even starting to get me. One thing—no matter how much this guy may look like Elvis, he couldn't have had Elvis' eyes. They're his and his alone, because this guy doesn't have Elvis' soul. I was, by the way, followed through the desert. Then coming back, I had a flat tire. Tomorrow I've got to run him to the tailor, run him to Priscilla. and he will probably write to you, too, before the night is over. Unless he's too weary. And I'll have to get that to you. See why I have no time for the little, unimportant things in life. Working!

I still think I ought to dump Kit right in his bed and knock their heads together! So help me I would have done it for the hell of it, to see what would happen, only the time is not right and far be it from me to break the rules. Maybe then El would forget Prissy and Kit would get her mind off a certain Welsh citizen. Well—I wish the time would hurry up! Lots of things need fixing up.

Until later when El will undoubtedly write.

Marlon

Marlon is becoming obsessed with the notion that an Elvis double is roaming around Los Angeles and causing trouble for his friend, and he thinks this double has fathered a child with Priscilla.

October 19, 1969

One of the most disheartening things about being a celebrity is the intense media scrutiny, much of it fictional, or mostly so. Newsworthy individuals have fewer legal protections against slander and libel, so they are easy targets. During their careers, Marlon, Harry, Elvis and Tom Jones were no exceptions.

In this letter to Carmen, Marlon vents his frustration over some recent libelous magazine articles about Tom. Unfortunately, he had shown the articles to Kit, who apparently had told her friend Carmen Montez that Marlon was trying to diminish her affection for Tom. Whether true or not, Marlon uses this letter to explain why he did this. In the end, he goes a bit overboard in praising the positive qualities of Tom.

Almost as an aside, perhaps because violence had become almost expected, Marlon reveals that another shot had been fired at Tom Jones.

Dear Carmen;

I talked to Tom today. He called to see if I'd gotten the letter and had given it to you. I told him I had and he said he had written another and sent it in Elvis' care and you should get it—or El should—by Wed. or Thurs. Apparently he has something on his mind. He also said he will call Elvis between one and two our time Wed. He tapes the final portion of Thurs. show about that time. I think Kit misunderstood my motive in showing her the magazines I let her have yesterday. I was not trying to down Tom. I'm not bringing him down in anyway, whatever smut is there does not come from Tom, it is in the minds of others who are using Tom for their own purposes. I showed her these articles because it's obvious that someone is out to get him in any way they can. If not by bullets, by tearing him down, and in my opinion, that one article was really hitting mighty low.

Also, Elvis brought up a good point. Strange that the same magazine should print an article on Tom and me in the same issue. What happened to me would have been very funny, indeed, if they'd have told it without all the other insinuations. It wasn't exactly funny to me, but in a movie it would have been hilarious. I've never tried to play Santa Claus again!

Getting back to Tom, I told him about that article. I really advised him to sue the magazine. He laughed and said "How can I sue them? You've got to prove things in a lawsuit and how the hell am I going to do that unless I do a public strip tease." And he's right. They hit him where he can't fight back. I'm beginning to think you Gemini people are just too well endowed for your own good.

On top of everything else someone took a pot shot at Tom the night before last as he was getting into his car. It missed him by a mile, but he felt it was meant to be a warning that he hasn't escaped though he's an ocean away. The police said it was some fan's jealous boyfriend, but Tom doesn't believe it.

Anyway, in this sense I will defend Tom with true conviction! I hate to see a smear campaign waged against him because he's truly above such things. He sometimes gets away with murder on stage because he does it with that twinkle in his eye. He seems to let go and do what he really feels. And it has a ring of honesty about it. Off stage he's honest, doesn't pull any punches but I've never found him vulgar or in bad taste either in speech, manner or thought. He doesn't go along with today's way of thinking, hippies and orgies, and as he says, "turning the world upside down to suit their own morality."

For someone so "In" he is out of it, and it's a refreshing change. He's not temperamental, he works very hard and he's never cross with anyone. I'd like to see the guy who wrote that article work as hard as Tom and not perspire. He's got high blood pressure besides and he can't help that any more than he can help the way he's built. Or anyone else can. If Tom and I ever get into a personal battle, and one day we just might, we'd shake hands before and after and it would be quite fair and square because that's the way he is. And I hate to see him get some of the dirty deals he's gotten only for trying to help Elvis, who needs all of our help. So that's my stand, and I want you to know, and also Kit, that I am not persecuting Tom. He made no mention of our previous conversation in his letter to me, so let it stay there.

Marlon

December 8, 1969

Marlon seems to have a stream of concerns about his friends. In this letter he worries about Kit's depression and Tom Jones's shortness of breath. His apparent sincerity in praising Tom's recent TV performance indicates that his spat over the relationship between Tom and Kit is mostly resolved.

Dear Carmen;

I'm feeling just a little concerned for all of us tonight. I think the only one I'm not worried about to some degree is Harry. At least as far as I know he is all right. Elvis, of course is first on the list. However, Parker is back in town, I've talked to him. In fact, he is the one who told me about Elvis' picture opening in one to 3 weeks, depending upon the theatre's current booking. So now that you know he's here, he made you a promise, and by damn I want to see the bastard keep it!

Then I've had some problems of my own. I'm moving from the valley house. I'll be out Monday a week. The 15th. Then I always feel concerned when you're sick. We need you—and besides—things are bad enough without me being cheated out of your fabulous spaghetti!

And Kit is quite depressed and unhappy. I guess she's been tied down to something all of her life. Ill health in childhood, then her mother's illness, a job that didn't suit her, and now a child who needs her. And by darn if I don't think she really goes for Tom Jones! You know I thought she was crazy, and he was kidding around. Now I'm not so sure. All I can say is she better get on it and latch onto him pretty quick if she means it—before some other gal does. I'd of thought Elvis was more her type—but maybe they're too alike—more like a brother and sister—and perhaps she needs someone opposite—yet in sympathy and congenial with her own background. Perhaps it takes one Welshman to understand another, and the Mexicans, the Negroes, and the Frenchmen like me just aren't really her cup of tea. [Referring to himself as a Frenchman seems to be an inside joke derived from the fact that Brando spoke French—badly, as he often said.]

Then Tom tonight scared the devil out of me. He and Gordon Mills came by about 11 to have some tea with me and Tom suddenly couldn't get his breath. I noticed one time on the show he was straining for breath, and he sounded like he'd been running when I'd talked to him earlier. He got up to get a glass of water and started gasping again. I asked him what was wrong, and he said he'd been getting a sharp pain in his chest off and on all night.

He'd had a physical he said, right before he left London, and was in tip top shape. It seemed to leave him and then before he could sit down again, he grabbed hold of the edge of the table and hung on so hard his knuckles went white and started gasping and turning blue. Gordon slapped him on the back and that only choked him up.

I got on the phone and called a doctor to come quick, but whatever it was passed gradually before the doctor came, leaving him very exhausted but all right. And the doctor could find nothing wrong. He'd had 2 glasses or so of champagne, he said, between shots or acts, but the doctor said it wasn't that unless—there's still drugs in his system and wine doesn't mix with it.

He did a beautiful job on "Yesterday", didn't he? It's sometimes hard to tell if certain songs are down deep within Tom, or if he's getting down inside him. He so perfectly, so beautifully merges with his music at times that listening and watching becomes an experience rather than diversion. once in a while I catch an expression—about the mouth and chin—a look Kit gets at times. And this sort of startles me.

I wish some things were in my power to work out. Maybe they're in yours. How I hope.

—— Marlon

P.S. Just talked to Harry this morning. He, at least, is fine. He saw part of Tom's show between his own numbers last night. He left the set on backstage, and he said he missed his own cue when Tom was doing "Yesterday". He said he couldn't tear himself away from the set. He, too, said Tom did a magnificent job last night. There are some songs Tom sings, and very well, too, but as Harry said, there are others he seems to jump inside of and make part of himself. These he doesn't sing, he lives them. Harry said he felt Tom's heart was "aching in every part of him" when he did that song. Harry added "If a man's soul were ever put on film, that was it." I don't know exactly what he was thinking, or who he had in his mind, but he looked like he was really hurting, and I've never seen any singer put so much of himself into his work.

January 1970

Marlon had lobbied hard for Elvis to change managers. He had proposed that Gordon Mills, who managed Tom Jones, pick up Elvis. According to this post-Christmas letter to Carmen, that relationship could not be worked out.

Marlon makes an interesting comment about Harry Belafonte: "Now Harry is back, and oh, boy—clash! Sweet, subtle—nevertheless darts and daggers flying!" The reason for any conflict between these old friends and human rights activists can only be Kit. This mystery woman seems to intoxicate and motivate every man who meets her.

Dear Carmen;

Well, here's hoping the 70's will be better for us all! Thank you for the cuff links and I hope you didn't find my gift too useless or absurd! I can't say why I like that set but for some reason it intrigued me. It's great for Kahlua or liquors at a small diner. I guess I really went with whim this year! Kit did all right.

Hope you made out as well with Santa Claus. I think he got stuck in my chimney this year! y the looks of things, Mr.

Jones still hasn't forgotten about Kit. I didn't care too much for his new record myself. There are times when I don't think Tom's in good taste. Like the times he slows down those rotating hips and concentrates on the pelvis. He brings down the house but with his voice and ability he doesn't need those kind of tricks.

Anyway, he has a smart manager. Too bad Mills couldn't handle Elvis, too. Only I realize he would never get any sleep if he had both, plus Humperdinck. Mills certainly isn't stupid—he gets 40% of Tom, and 40% of Englebert. He ends up with 80%, and they each have 60%.

Love that yellow sweater you gave Kit! Blue and yellow are my colors, you know. Funny, all of us—Elvis, Tom and me, prefer blue as our color. Harry likes orange or red, then blue. And Elvis and Tom take red as second preference. You are to the blue side with Turquoise, and Kit's for red. That must mean we're all one big compatible family!

Well, this holiday's been a tiring one for me. I've had my finger in several campaigns, and I've had Chris on and off, and then my sister Frances came here from Illinois and is staying here until next Fri. Now Harry is back, and oh, boy—clash! Sweet, subtle—nevertheless darts and daggers flying! So I'll write later.

Have a happy 1970.

Marlon

March 1970

This short letter was written to Carmen early in 1970. Originally, I had misdated this letter to 1968, but new information has helped me correct that error. The letter is pivotal in two ways. First, it reveals for the first time that Priscilla Presley knew about Elvis's relationship with Carmen Montez. As Brando describes the scene, Priscilla gave him a letter addressed to Carmen and asked him to deliver it. For years, I wondered what Priscilla had written to Elvis's secret confidante. Two months after my book's publication, a reader of *Letters from Elvis* reported that he possessed that handwritten note and its envelope. The full text of Priscilla's note will be presented in a later section entitled *The Briefcase*.

Second, Marlon explains an eerie premonition—"a strange, nameless fear for Elvis." Within a few weeks, that premonition would be proven correct in the most brutal manner. A recently discovered letter from Elvis to Carmen may provide the answer to the mystery. A transcript of that letter is also presented in the section entitled *The Briefcase*.

Dear Carmen;

I talked to Elvis earlier and he said he had wanted to give

you a copy of the single of "If I Can Dream" so you wouldn't always have to put on the big album to listen to it. Also, he wrote the back-up tune from that picture of his. In the confusion he had forgotten to give it to you. But he had left me with the key to the kitchen door and had taken the electric off the gate, and had padlocked it and also gave me the key to that.

His cousin and her brother-in-law left with him, and no one is there at all. So the maid comes to me for the key on Mondays, and he asked me to keep an eye out, especially on the cars. So he said while I check around today, I should take a copy of "If I Can Dream" for you.

I was coming back from this errand, approaching my house, and who should I see coming toward me but Priscilla. She had a cab waiting for her, informed me she and Lisa were on their way to Memphis and she had been looking for me. She shoved an envelope in my hand, smiled sweetly, and disappeared into the cab after telling me to give it to the "proper party". When I looked at it, it was addressed as you see, and she was gone. So—I didn't know what else to do, other than give it to you. I'm anxiously waiting for word from you. Please let me know if there's anything I have to do. I know where Elvis will be tonight, and I can telephone his trailer if it's anything urgent. I've been puzzled and rather upset all day. Let me know.

Marlon

P.S. Carmen—for a week now—I've had a funny—a strange, nameless fear for Elvis. I don't know what it is, but I'm afraid of something. I wish you knew what it might be.

July 11, 1970

This revealing letter makes clear that sometime in 1970, perhaps in February or March, Priscilla again had become pregnant, a fact never announced to the public. Despite having been taken to the hospital, she loses the baby.

Marlon is correct when he writes, "I have a pretty good idea that someone made an assault on his [Elvis's] person, or his wife." The details of another attack by the Katzman gang are presented in *Letters from Elvis* (pages246-249) and are drawn mostly from Elvis's confidential letters to Carmen Montez. In brief, two Katzman thugs had broken into Elvis's Palm Springs home while he and Priscilla were there mostly alone. The two men, who had been present at the brutal abduction and torture in 1968, delivered threats at gunpoint and physically jostled Priscilla, who was pregnant.

The fiction of Elvis having been incapable of existing without support and being perpetually accompanied by members of the Memphis mafia is a legend fostered by many of those close to him who wrote books intended to show how Elvis could not live without them. As the Montez letters show, he was fully capable of taking care of himself, though he sometimes called on friends for help. Why would he do this if he always had "minders" accompanying him?

At this point, Marlon does not know the wretched details of this latest Katzman assault, so he quickly changes the subject to movie business matters.

Dear Carmen:

Something has happened to Elvis, but I don't know just what is wrong. He finally reached me from St. John's hospital where he took Priscilla. He says she's having what appears to be false labor but it's possible she could have the baby early. He wouldn't tell me exactly what happened, just asked me to "please come and be with me" and he seemed all choked up. I asked him if he was all right and at that his voice broke and he said "Oh, God, oh God they won't ever Let me alone," and he sounded at the breaking point.

Maybe your letter will help. I'll come back and get it after I make sure he's all right. I'll try to persuade him to go to my place because at this stage this with Priscilla could go on all night. I'll know more when I get there. I told him this. That I'd had word from you that there was no attempt on his life. He said "That's right. She's right. They didn't make an attempt on my life," so I have a pretty good idea that someone made an assault on his person, or his wife.

It's something that's got him shook and he can't manage to talk about it yet. So I'm a little "shook" myself. Just in brief, I think you should try to postpone Burton's [actor Richard Burton] coming in until the following week if you can. Of course, that's the time Tom will be here, too. Maybe that would even work for the good, though.

Joe's knocking himself out on this but he told me this morning, without help he cannot possibly make it by Friday. The next week, yes, but he has two important things that has to be done for Elvis this week and aside from that, he's giving it all his time. But he won't do it unless he does it properly, and a week is just too little time. He wanted to re-space it, etc., but I told him to do is as it's written, because it would run into too many pages for copying, at this time.

We are fortunate to have a professional typist, and when it's finished I'm sure it will be done right because he's very meticulous. It will still be ready for Tom, so if you can put off Burton for one week, we'll be set. I feel like it's good luck in the end. Elvis is putting a little into it too, by sacrificing his convenience for a couple of weeks. I'll get your letter later, and maybe El will open up to you if he can't to me. Whatever it is, it's better he gets it out in the open.

Say a Prayer for Elvis and I'll pray Burton will have a change of schedule.

Marlon

July 15, 1970

A few days after finding out about the latest assault, Marlon has learned some frightening details. According to Marlon, Priscilla had refused to believe the events of the 1968 kidnapping and torture of her husband, finding them too implausible. The vicious invasion of her Palm Springs home, however, persuaded her that Elvis had been telling the truth.

I find this revelation gratifying. That even Elvis's wife could not believe the facts of her husband's abduction and sexual assault, even after Marlon—a participant in the kidnapping and rescue of Elvis—had verified the story, helps me understand how so many readers of *Letters from Elvis* cannot believe what had happened. For Priscilla, it took being attacked personally by two of the same men to see the truth.

This letter reveals some additional facts about the Palm Springs assault that Priscilla told Marlon.

I'm short on paper today, so here's your envelope back! Excuse it! My goodness, we do write alike! I can hardly tell the difference. [Our handwriting experts, however, had no difficulty identifying numerous differences in their script.]

Dear Carmen;

Thanks for your letter. I'm very pleased that Harry is keeping in close touch. I've heard so many good things about his work in "Angel Levine" [1970 movie *The Angel Levine* starring Harry and Zero Mostel.] I'm very glad because, if you'll remember, you and I were among the first to believe in his ability in this field. Will you try to let me know about how much luck you've had about Las Vegas, by at least Thursday? Otherwise I'm afraid Elvis will start buying up Hotels or Motels in Las Vegas!

Seriously, I wouldn't put it past him to make a whole week's reservations if he had to. He's determined and won't be stopped. He said he'd do it if it was the last thing he ever did. Then he laughed and said it may be. Elvis thought a motel might be more convenient, and less conspicuous. By now he'd probably settle for a boarding house. I have to laugh every time I think about Elvis and the belts he wants for Vegas.

Before all this trouble happened, the day I took him to the tailor, I came back for him and was looking around the shop in Beverly Hills. Elvis was trying on some suede belts which his tailor thought he could have beaded. He asked me what I thought about the color of one of them, and he turned around so I could see, and there, stamped right on the back of the belt, just where he couldn't see it, was, in big chalky white letters: "Made in Mexico". He nearly broke his neck trying to see what I was laughing about. Don't worry - they can't pull that "dope" bit on me. As long as they don't go too far with Elvis. That's all I'm worried about.

It must have been pretty bad for him last week. Priscilla didn't believe what happened to him before. Well, I guess she does now. She said they worked him over pretty bad, it was frightening and unbelievably sadistic. She was even crying, so she must have been afraid. She said she didn't believe such things could happen, she didn't realize anyone could be hurt so badly that way.

She even told me she chased after me that time because she had the idea that Elvis and I "had something going" and she wanted to break it up and shock him. I can't believe that girl's mind, but at least she admits she can't believe now that Elvis could have ever been a party to that sort of thing. She must be from Missouri instead of Tennessee, with her, seeing is believing. She said she still doesn't know why they didn't kill her and Elvis both.

Pris was really in shock because they told Elvis if he made one move to get up or even move his head unless he was told, they'd not only blast him but cut her and take the baby. They held a gun on him all the time so he didn't dare make a move or a sound. She said they rammed the gun down his throat until he was nearly choking on it, and that isn't the only place they rammed it.

Pris needed a good shock, and if this doesn't do it nothing ever will. It's only too bad she's come to realize these things a little too late. Elvis will forgive, because that's the way he is. But there's just too much to forget. He's an idealist and the moment he starts remembering, the old hurt creeps in. It's gone beyond the point of return. He may give in to his heart and weaken at times, but his mind tells him not to take any more.

I've got to give up for now. I cut my hand on a piece of broken china from the cups El broke. I did it this morning, but now that I'm writing it's bothering me. So I'll say so long for now.

Marlon

July 18, 1970

Marlon reveals a few more details about the Palm Springs home invasion and relieves the darkness of the event by telling Carmen a humorous story about Elvis.

Dear Carmen;

Elvis said to thank you for the letter and returning the record. He's going to stay here until he feels he can make it back to Vegas. I don't like him up there in this weakened, depressed state. He's a little weaker right now than he was this morning. He met up with a hot tamale who wouldn't let go -of him! Tarita came home with her girlfriend Tondelayo, who is believe it or not, half Spanish, half Russian, Tahitian born and raised, and she speaks French mostly, with a little Spanish thrown in.

Joselyn drove them here, and the minute they came in, this chick spied Elvis asleep (at last) on the sofa. She had worked as a chorus dancer in "Stay Away, Joe" because she looks Indian. Seeing Elvis, her eyes got big as saucers, she ran over and kissed him (with Tahitian enthusiasm), he jumped nearly through my ceiling, then looked relieved to see it was nothing more than a helpless female.

So Joselyn and I went into the kitchen to make tea, and the next thing, Tarita came out and said I'd better come in and break it up because Tondelayo was half way to attaching our house guest. She was sitting on the poor guy, had latched onto his hair, the part that falls down, and wouldn't let go. His shirt was unbuttoned to his waist and he was yelling for her to cut it out, but she doesn't understand English. That chick was all over him, pulling his hair, he was yelling to me "How do you turn her off?" and I said try French and he didn't know any, so he tried Spanish, but all he could think of in Spanish was, "Si, Si".

I think this boy's in need of a few quick lessons in basic Spanish! Also, a suit of armor would help. Right now he's of the opinion that these Latins are "too much". At least the doctor told him to exercise his arm now. Man, that gal didn't care where she was or who was there. Poor El, waking up like that. I had to stop writing because Elvis collapsed. I knew it was coming. He was carrying a tray of ten cups into the kitchen for my wife. I heard a crash and stopped writing. He went out cold, fell in the broken china, cut a bad gash right in front of his left ear, and two little cuts, one over the left eyebrow. I had to call one of my doctors, who came and said he was suffering from exhaustion and has an extremely low blood count.

The doctor left sedation and if Elvis won't take it I'm afraid he's going to be hospitalized. If that silly girl had let him sleep, then he may have been all right. Right now I don't want to see him in any hospital if it can be avoided. I just want to be certain the same person comes out.

I called Priscilla at Elvis' request to tell her he couldn't go to see her today as he'd promised, and she told me pretty much of what had happened. Poor Elvis. It's bad enough but keeping it all in the way he has—he's got a lot more fortitude than many people know.

Pris was crying because they tore her negligee. She said,

"But it was the one I had on my honeymoon, my beautiful honeymoon negligee." Well, I think they also did a good job of tearing up her beautiful husband, and he went along with the honeymoon so I think a few more tears would be in order for him. I'm sorry, but she still gripes me!

Well, I'd better see my wife about a few things and try to get some food down El so he can get some rest. I think we all need it—you and me, too. I've got to have a good talk with Tom and brief him when he comes.

Marlon

July 19, 1970

Marlon explains that Elvis believes the child Priscilla is carrying is his, but Marlon has doubts. Elvis, he writes, really wants to have this child—perhaps because he still feels responsible for the death of another child, mentioned earlier. We assume from known history that no more children will be born to Priscilla, of course, but the letters do not explain when or how this baby died.

In reading Brando's letters to Carmen, I am continually astonished at how obsessed Marlon is with Elvis's welfare. It seems like he is insinuating himself into Elvis's life in a remarkably intimate way seldom seen in men.

Dear Carmen;

Well, if they're trying to wear Elvis down, they're doing a great job of it! Down and out. The poor kid hasn't slept since Sat. night—about 60 some hours right now. He was talking on my phone today, laying on his stomach, talking - - the next minute he'd fallen asleep. So I went and got a pillow and tried to take the phone away and turn him over. He jumped up like he'd been shot, those bleary eyes going wild and all ready to defend himself. So he's apparently scared to death to go to sleep. If you could only make one of your visits to him at night when all is quiet, you may be able to calm him. Right now, Elvis needs a mother. He needs some trusting, loving arms around him. And try as I may to be a friend, and a brother, I'll never make the grade as a mother!

I've noticed a lot of things. He's hurting. I notice the way he moves, and it isn't only his head. They're trying to wear him down, humiliate him, take the heart out of him, so when they're good and ready, he will go to the slaughter without a fight. The only reason he's fighting is for Lisa. He wouldn't go through all this, Carmen, if it weren't for that child. And now—it's strange, and I see it now—somehow this child is important to Elvis. I can't quite explain it—maybe he's convinced himself it is his—I don't know. But it's gotten to be important. I had to call Priscilla today and tell her Elvis didn't have the strength to make it down. He'd of tried, but he couldn't even hold a razor to shave. If he doesn't get some sleep between now and the time I go to sleep, I'm seriously going to slip him a couple of sleeping pills in some milk. Once he gets some rest maybe he will feel different. This time he closed up, even to me.

Whatever went on down there must have been pretty rough. Priscilla was in shock for almost three days. She was in false labor for almost 24 hours, then she went into hysteria and the doctor thought he'd have to take the baby. She's calming down with sedation now, but Elvis here has had neither sedation nor sleep.

He can't go back to Las Vegas or anywhere like this. He was going to hire two plain clothes security men to go with him wherever he goes, but that would be a tip-off he suspects something, and they could always be bought! Unfortunately, he can trust no one except you and me and Tom, maybe one or two more. Maybe.

I'm really afraid for Elvis, Carmen. His back is to the wall. He's going down fighting but he'd might as well have half a dozen guns pointed at his head. Fighting doesn't do a bit of good against his odds. Well—if he'd only stayed away from Priscilla. His heart always leads him into trouble.

I'll be in touch. Elvis is all yours. Good luck. I can't handle him when he closes up like this. If there is anything I can do, I'm here.

Marlon

I had to show you these pictures of El as a child. I'd give them to you but I'm going to blackmail him with those! Some thirty years later the same bewildered look is on his face!

January 1972

In this first letter of 1972 to Carmen, Marlon sends warm greetings. The way he writes about the season, though, it seems to have been a rather "blue Christmas." After a few years of intense honesty and intimate sharing, this letter seems quite businesslike and casual, almost as if Brando is starting to withdraw from the relationship.

Dear Carmen:

It seems like we have been close for many, many Christmases now. I really ought to scold you for spending so much on me. I know how things are, you know. But I must say I love the cufflinks. I've worn them ever since Christmas, so you know I like them. I was somewhat uncomfortable over Christmas. I had a bad bump on my chin and I couldn't eat much Christmas dinner after my wife cooked it, so we decided to celebrate "little Christmas" to make up for it. So I guess we all felt pretty down and out over Christmas.

Look for "The Nightcomers" to be out soon. The "Godfather" of course will be premiered around Easter. Elvis seemed a little blue. I guess he was worried about you and Tom, too. But he seems to be in better spirits since the new year. I think that of all of us, Harry had the best Christmas. At least he said he spend a peaceful day with his children, playing in the park in the snow, and then his ex-wife send dinner over since their two children were with Harry.

Also, Carmen, Tom said to be sure to say thank you to you. He was going to write you a note because Kit and he were to have lunch together Sat. But now she has had a change of plans, and I don't think I'll get out to see Tom right now, so he can't get a letter to you. But he said I should be sure to thank you for him when I wrote. Well—nothing new just now.

I hope 1972 will be a kind and generous lady to all of us. My wife also thanks you for her gift, and I'm so happy you like my little remembrance. I thought it would remind you of me, and some of the memories we've shared throughout the years.

Take good care of yourself, and get well quickly, and I'm keeping my fingers crossed for Kit's script, for both your sakes. You know, I surely miss having El near. It's lonesome up here since he's gone.

Well, Carmen, you know what I wish you—what I've always wished you. So have a happy, bright prosperous New Year.

Lots of Love,

Marlon

June 15, 1972

In this next Brando letter, delivered five months after the Christmas letter, Brando infers that he and Carmen have not been communicating regularly. Brando writes this letter in response to an unexpected letter from Carmen, the contents of which I do not have. The first half of 1972 has been full of financial, career and marital difficulties for Brando, as he explains.

The letter has a sweet, reminiscent tone—until Marlon slips in another note of terror without hardly raising an eyebrow. It seems that fear and dread of the future continue to haunt Elvis just as the ghost of Jeni haunts Marlon.

Dear Carmen:

You don't know how surprised I was when I got your letter. I didn't even know you knew my situation. I really hesitated to take it from you, Carmen. I was afraid you gave up something you needed for me. It's such a silly thing for me to be in such a position. I guess you understand why I couldn't tell Elvis or Tom. Elvis looks up to me, and I guess in a way Tom respects me and I feel so foolish. But everything is tied up until Jan 2nd, and then I have lawsuits from Movita and Anna, and a settlement on Tarita, plus a former lawyer is suing me, and I'm in for it over back-taxes.

Anyway, I wouldn't have taken it if it weren't that I hated to give my car up. I'd have had to buy a second hand one to get around, and it's a funny thing, Carmen, but when I had an old jalopy and everybody knew I was box-office, nobody said anything except that I was eccentric. Now, they'd say I was broke. So I not only thank you, Carmen, but I appreciate it almost as much as I do our lasting friendship.

It's been a lot of years, hasn't it, my friend? How the time has gone and we've all had our ups and downs. Well, now that I'm single again guess you'll be hearing more from me. It was sort of hard to write sometimes with my wife there. I didn't want to have to hide letters, and yet, since we've known each other so long, and confided in each other, it was sometimes easier for me to write to you than to talk to her. Yet I miss her. I really thought she was calling my bluff when she threatened divorce. There were several reasons why I couldn't give in to her and she didn't understand. Well, that's all over now. Now Chris will have to stay with my sister Frances again. And just when I'd legally won the battle. The house suddenly seems lonely.

I'm glad Elvis moved back near me. He's away now but it will help having a good friend close when he comes back. I'm greatly concerned for Elvis. I got a call from him today. He had a dream with you last night. You came to him on the desert wearing a turquoise night gown. You told him to have his car checked and then you disappeared. This morning he asked Charlie Hodge if the car needed a check-up and Charlie said the points were the only trouble spot. Elvis had him take it into the garage and the mechanic found a time bomb under the hood set to go off at 6:40 P.M.

Someone knew Elvis had to be at a radio station on the outskirts of Las Vegas at 7 P.M. He would have left at 6:30 and it takes about twenty minutes to drive it. He says hereafter he will take a taxi in town. I guess you heard he wants to back Tom to help make up for what happened with Gordon. Gordon is really in the middle now. I'm sorry for him but it's really hurting Tom, professionally and personally. Tom really counted on Gordon for guidance and wisdom. That old man really knows how to hurt.

I guess Tom and Kit have it pretty bad for each other. I must admit I didn't think it would last but it's been nearly three years now and they can't seem to live without each other. I sometimes think she lives from meeting to meeting. She called him her tower of strength the other day and I must admit she's a new woman since she has him. I hope she never loses him. Funny for me to say that—but I see the difference he's made in her life. But that throat sounds pretty bad. He needs you close, too. So do I these days.

Thanks again, with all my heart, my understanding friend.

Marlon

Summer 1972

In this undated letter sent to Carmen sometime during the summer of 1972, Brando tells Carmen that the Elvis "double" continues to cause trouble for Elvis and Priscilla. I have learned that Elvis Presley Enterprises had used doubles as decoys to bait frenzied fans away from Elvis. Some theorists have speculated that lookalike relatives of Elvis may have been performing occasionally as Elvis. And about this time, Johnny Harra, known as the first and greatest Elvis Tribute Artist, was beginning to make a name for himself.

Johnny Harra, often called the world's first Elvis Tribute Artist (ETA) and the greatest Elvis impersonator.

Any of these individuals may have been the double mentioned by Brando. In this letter, Marlon reveals a plot to identify and neutralize the troublemaker. Marlon's obsession with this individual remains unabated.

Since the publication of *Letters from Elvis*, I have been drawn into relationships with many other knowledgeable people, Presley family members, Elvis acquaintances and researchers. I have been given access to a large collection of DNA samples voluntarily provided by members of all branches of the Vernon Presley and Gladys Smith family trees. I have investigated multiple claimants who believe they are offspring or other close relatives of Elvis. And I have examined the claims of numerous Elvis theorists.

I have finally uncovered a solution to the problem that most likely consumed Brando—Elvis's "double." When I have thoroughly verified my research, the next book will delve deeply into this phenomenon and deliver a story that is even more astonishing than the one revealed in the letters from Elvis, Brando, Belafonte and Tom Jones.

I believe that Marlon Brando had stumbled onto something that was in fact just a small and obscure clue to a much larger mystery. As that old TV series *The X-Files* once said: "The truth is out there."

Dear Carmen;

Well, I had an unexpected break today that may help Elvis. My wife and her girlfriend were watching Art Linkletter's show on television and Tarita called me to come quick and look at this fellow who looked so much like Elvis. I came in and behold—I know this was the same guy. Furthermore, he was modeling western clothing for Nudie the tailor who is Elvis' tailor!

The tailor is Nudie's Rodeo Tailor at 5015 Lankershim Dr. in North Hollywood. I called the T.V. station and they referred me to Linkletter's office and after lunch I caught up with Art himself, who told me the model's name is Ronnie Bisset (not sure of spelling) and the show was taped several months ago and someone had tried to hold back the release but they finally showed it anyway. Now we know the name he is going by professionally and I'm going to do some checking. This proves he's hung around in that area, that's probably where he's gotten his expensive clothes, and he probably does modeling and played in combos to pick up extra money.

Parker probably saw him modeling over there and decided to groom him to look like Elvis. The owner of the shop is an ex-fighter and I doubt very much that he's in on it. Although who knows? Carmen, if you should happen to be in the neighborhood over there one day, why don't you just casually happen to go by and look around the store. See what you might come up with. This guy's picture may be there in some of the clothes—or something may come up where—I don't know what might happen, but I feel the fates are trying very hard to help us.

I want this guy exposed for the sake of El's reputation as well as his life. The guy's trying his hardest to ruin both. I'd go snooping but they'd know me—and who knows this guy may still be working there. He may have been a clerk-model for a while. El has all his western and western movie clothes there. They even showed a full-length picture of Elvis on the T.V. screen. Let me know any thoughts you may have on this. I'll wait to hear what you think. Wait till I tell El. With this the guy can be traced. All we need now is evidence of what he's doing. I only wish the snoopy news people could get on his trail now. That would really throw a scare into someone! Let me hear what you think now.

Marlon

His social security is probably under this name.

Mid-August 1972

Carmen Montez had never met Elvis Presley face-to-face. Their relationship had been developed through correspondence and, rarely, by telephone. At last, in August of 1972, Elvis decides it's time for them to get together. Since Carmen has never seen Elvis perform live, he attempts to get her tickets to a show in Vegas. Carmen and Kit make it to the performance, but fate prevents Carmen from meeting Elvis after the show as expected. This letter is Marlon's account of the preparations.

Dear Carmen;

I really shouldn't be telling you this, but Elvis has worked so hard by phone all this morning trying to make you reservations for Las Vegas the end of next month, and I felt so sorry for him that I had to tell you. He wants to surprise you and have everything all set up, and he can't use his name, so he's in trouble. He said today he learned what it's like not to be Elvis Presley. He spent two and a half hours on that phone, and something like a fifty-dollar phone bill and they just won't make a reservation for a Sat. night unless it's for someone of importance, or someone known there.

So it occurred to me that you may know someone who could help you. Elvis will pay for it, it's just getting it for the night of Sat. Aug. 29. He's trying to get a double room with twin beds (for you and Kit—or you and your "girlfriend" because he senses Kit in some way is associated with you.) He's already worked something out about the show and says there's no problem there and he intends to pay for that part. But after a drive like that you'll need a room, and he would have even paid for a room for Fri. and Sat. but they won't hold it even if it's paid for, if you're not there on Fri. They keep the Fri. money, and refund for Sat.

Meanwhile he's still going to work on it, but time is getting short and I thought if I told you, you may know someone who can use their influence where he cannot at this moment. He even tried downtown, tried to get a suite at the El Cortez. The girl on the phone there told him "Do you know you sound a great deal like Elvis Presley?" He told her "Well, honey you'd sound just as bad if you had been on the phone all morning." After that he tried to disguise his voice, so if you come up with a reservation made by a china man, you'll know the source. This boy's getting good with the dialects.

After last night (Kit said she told you) it's a wonder he has the presence of mind to do anything. It threw me. I'm going to fight this thing if it takes every penny I have. Well, don't tell Elvis just yet—he's going to be disappointed if he can't do it himself but I figure if you check into it, too, it's better that way, then if he can't manage it, he'd feel even worse, and eventually he will tell you anyway, so an ace in the hole has its value. If you come up with anything, I'll suggest that you have friends also, and we'll work out the payment. If he's up there, I'll give it to you until he gets back. So that isn't the problem. Elvis is like a kid sometimes and I just hate to see him always hurt. Tom gets close to you, so does Harry, but poor Elvis can't make it. I hope I didn't do wrong to break confidence. I figure it could help, not hurt.

Until later, Marlon

1972

There are two things to understand before reading this letter. First, I have not been able to date this letter more definitively than 1972. Second, Marlon has been channeling, or thinks he has been channeling, the spirit of Elvis's deceased girlfriend, "Jeni." He states that this channeling puts a great strain on him. Later, I will present some of these channeled letters.

Dear Carmen:

Excuse me that I haven't answered you for so long. My wife kept me busy, then Elvis came back, and this is the first chance I had to be alone to write. I like to be by myself when I write to you. Don't worry about me, Carmen. I'm all right. A little tired. It's mainly the things like Elvis' problems that keep me on edge. I think he's still going to have trouble with that Parker girl. Her lawyer's a tough one. He's not going to give up on a gold mine that easily. But I don't want to discourage Elvis' optimism.

Too, it's a strain when Jeni uses me for communication. It's very hard afterward but it's important to either you or Elvis, or maybe Kit, so it has to be done. Otherwise she wouldn't come to me.

Then there are the outside troubles: the taxes and financial matters. I haven't been able to break even all year, yet I have to keep up a front. Otherwise, I'm feeling pretty good. Not the way I'd like to be, but there were many times when it was worse.

Also, the doctor is watching Tarita [Tarita Teriipaia, Marlon's third wife] very closely. There's a chance she could lose this baby. [She did.] So my biggest problems are mental.

Kit said you went over to the tailor's the other day. I'm anxious to hear your report and your feelings. I really wish that guy could be exposed for the imposter he is. I'm still checking and little by little I find things out. He played off and on with a combo at the Western place over there in the Valley. He hung around and got familiar with the musicians and then sat in. Then they called him to fill in once in a while when someone got sick. Seems he plays several instruments, none exceptionally, so I am told.

Well, my wife just told me I have to get my beauty's sleep. Do you think it will help? I'll keep you informed, and I am very glad Elvis came home. I'm proud of our boy! Take care and I'll wait to hear from you soon.

Marlon

Jeni Letter 1

I have not dated the "Jeni Letters," which Marlon considered to be his channeling of the spirit of Elvis's deceased girlfriend, Jeni. In these letters, "Jeni" refers to Kit, aka Joi Sommers, as "Cathy." This is confusing, but Cathy is the young screenwriter's real name—the others were pseudonyms or nicknames.

I have had an expert handwriting analyst review these "channeled" letters. Though physically written by Marlon Brando, the handwriting clearly shows that a different personality altogether has influenced the writing. There are distinctive differences in Marlon's handwriting when Jeni is "coming through" him. It's spooky to see it on the page.

A highly visible example of a handwriting difference is the way Brando crosses his "t's." In the image below, we see multiple crossbars in a Brando exemplar made when he is not channeling.

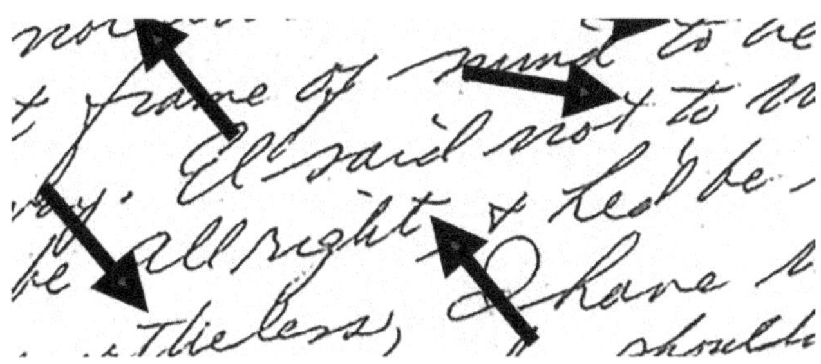

A non-channeling example of Brando handwriting shows a characteristic horizontal crossing on each t.

An example of Brando's handwriting while channeling Jeni shows markedly different t-crossings. Notice how the "t's" in this "Jeni" letter form "X's." To a Graphoanalyst, this indicates that the writer has been influenced by the death of someone. In this unusual case, that "someone" may be Jeni herself since she had previously died.

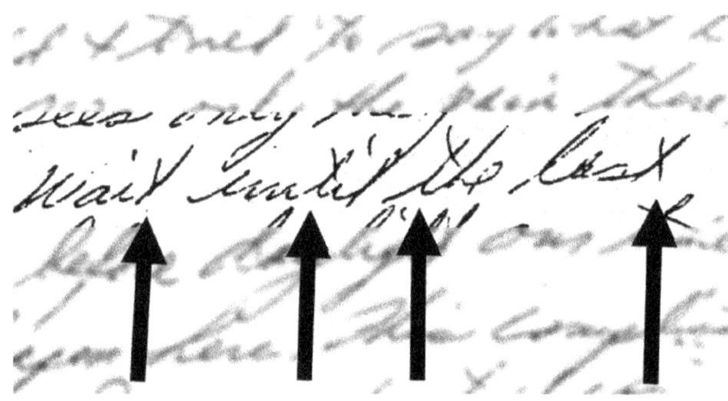

Wait until the last

An example of Brando's handwriting while channeling Jeni.

The details of this handwriting analysis are provided in *Letters from Elvis* (pages 94-96.) For the first time in print, however, the full text of four of these "Jeni" letters is presented here.

In this first letter, Jeni explains that Tom and Cathy have had other lives together, which made their relationship in this life inevitable.

Dear Carmen

This is Jeni coming to you through Marlon. When he awakens Marlon will not recall anything I have dictated to him.

What happened with Tom and Cathy was really an accident. Elvis is the present, Tom is both the past and what lies ahead in the future. I saw some time ago the shadow of another man but I did not know he was the man. They were lovers from the past with a drawing so strong they cannot let go and their coming together is something that has happened and will continue to happen once in every several lifetimes, until each learns and understands what they have done wrong. When this happens they will be together from there on. It should not have occurred in this particular life cycle, and something can only come of it when he wants it and she faces wanting him, both at the same time. They shall go on searching for one another through as many lifetimes as it takes to finally discover their mistake made many centuries ago. Their roots are the same and while the spirit takes on many forms and nationalities, this case is rare because they've always had each other's blood, even in the lives where one has not touched the other, and that accounts for such a strong and tangible drawing.

When they have not been cousins, close or far, they have been brother and sister, with a close attachment for one another carried over from the times when they were cousins. The blood relationship is where the trouble originally entered, for they loved each other in olden times, many centuries before cousins were allowed to love in their country. This is what pulled them apart at the beginning, and though times have changed and laws are different, the fear became inbred and handed down along with the love, time and time again. While the love endured, the fear destroyed and this time Tom's soul was touched at a time when he particularly needed a love to ease the pain I still see within his heart. If people only knew and understood more about spiritual love and what life is really made of, there would be so much less jealousy. For love itself when it is genuine and unselfish is never wrong.

As much as Tom has loved one woman in this life, has given up on that love, and therefore loved and lost another - each time his love has been in all sincerity, and even now this other love also encircles him and will leave its mark on his life and his soul, even if he should never more in this life experience it. The beauty of true love is in the loving, for real love itself is never lost. It only takes on different forms. This is one of the great secrets of living that few people ever know. When these two discover that love cannot be destroyed by man because it will only go on and come out some other way if denied, then and only then will they find each other. For in God's time all who truly love will be brought together, for to Him love is timeless and universal, jealousy does not exist. The love of brother for brother, mother for child or friend for friend is just as vital as the love of man for woman. It is not God, but the world you live in that restricts and says whom you can love.

What was wrong in times gone by is now right in the eyes of man. It is sometimes very difficult to know where to respect and live by the laws of man and where to accept the gifts given by God. They sometimes conflict, or so it appears. Often because of the world, heaven is lost. What a shame it is, Carmen, that so often people run through other people's lives in the name of love when they have no business ever being there. The promiscuous ones with no love in their hearts for anyone but themselves. They take their greed and call it love, as Priscilla has done to Elvis. These are the ones who hurt God, the ones who abuse and misuse the precious gifts they could put to good use.

Tom has gone through a phase of searching that came with his sudden success, a period he would not have gone through had his wife been a different kind of woman. He is not a real ladies man even if they love him. This is only on the surface, not deep down with him. He is much too smart a man to deceive himself. His strength is in being honest with himself. This is something most people find hard. Tom is steady and dependable and what he really wants is one woman to show affection, a quiet woman but one affectionate as well as romantic, one who will share his life with him and dissolve that deep inner loneliness that seems to cling to him even though he won't admit it. The moral of life is to accept love without guilt. Guilt comes from man, not from God. It can destroy and to destroy a gift of God is the sin which must be undone. The power to obtain is within yourselves. Settle for nothing less than that which is the true motivation of each being. To know is one thing, to understand is another. I hope you understand.

Jeni

Jeni Letter 2

This is an extremely weird letter from Jeni, the spirit being channeled by Marlon Brando. It was written shortly after Tom had been in a serious car accident and was paralyzed in such a way that the medical team believed he was dead. The letter begins with Jeni's spiritual account of a nurse's aide who inadvertently saved Tom's life in an astonishing way.

At the top of the Jeni letter, Marlon scrawled a note to Carmen after he had regained control from Jeni.

Dear Carmelita;

Jeni was here. She handed me this and I have a faint feeling I may have written it because I seem to have lost time somewhere and I can't recall. But then right now I'm not sure what I am doing.

Marlon

Dear Carmen:

This is Jeni again. You can rest a little easier, help has come at long last through a young girl who works at the hospital as a nurse's aide. I've never prayed as hard for anyone on the face of earth except for my Elvis when he was so close to death. I roamed the hospital searching for a way to help. I knew they were going to have Mr. Jones moved because too many rumors had circulated and people were gathering around the door of the room where he was. I saw only curiosity in the hearts of most of the people there, except for the one young trainee. I knew she had truly admired Tom and in her heart she had wanted to go into that room but she was afraid. She had taken a key to the room with the idea of getting inside but she lacked the courage to use it. I stayed with her and prayed and did all in my power to silently guide her.

Finally she slipped inside when her chance came but I thought she never would go near him. She stood there inside the door for such a long time while I tried to will her to go closer and just pull back the sheet from his face. I think she was afraid and never would have except that she touched his hair where the sheet didn't reach, and when she took her hand away it was wet. She lifted the sheet then and when she saw his eyes were open she started to run for the door but I'd taken the key and locked her inside. The poor thing was in panic, and afraid of being caught there, for she would lose her job for certain. When she finally forced herself to look back at Tom she saw his eyes had filled with tears that wet his face. Then she touched his face and knew he was alive, hot with emotional pressure and the heat of the light burning overhead, and sopping wet all over.

She started to scream and ran to the door and banged on it until everybody came. All that time so needlessly wasted there has weakened him unnecessarily but still not to the point of death. It was a terror worse than dying for him, one few men fortunately ever know, and it brought back memories of the mine disaster for he was conscious and knew he was helpless and pretty much alone and unable to function for himself.

Now he is being examined and shortly he's going to be taken into surgery to try to relieve some of the pressure in the back of the neck. Those nerves control most of the body and on this depends whether or not he will regain the use of his muscular control. The operation will take about an hour and 15 minutes, and he will awaken from it about the mid-way portion of his show tonight. At this time he will regain the use of his fingers and feeling in the soles of the feet. The injured finger will be hurting but he will be under heavy sedation yet so it won't be too bad. Concentrate deeply during his show which was completed only hours before all this, and after it go to him so he will know he is not alone in his struggle.

It will be morning there and he will rest comfortably in the love of those who care. By the afternoon, his time, the middle of your night, his hands should start to awaken and he will have feeling in the toes and feeling should start returning to the left side of his face. The face, and any parts where the nerves are close to the surface, is very painful. The left side is going to be even worse because his left side was more drastically injured. At this time I only see the one portion of his face and his lips coming out of it. Not being able to move about or speak or even utter a sound makes it seen all the worse. So we will both have to work on him to try to help him as he gradually returns to himself. I feel he will. He has the strength and courage to make it. It will be a living hell but he will make it. It's going to keep him off his feet through to the end of the year even if he does progress rapidly. Weeks of pain lay ahead, and time lost in his work, and plans reshuffled.

When he returns here he may be a little more fatalistic for a time, pushing less, and letting more to chance. Therefore, despite all that has happened, you must not lag behind in your efforts to get to him or through to his manager. By late '70 or '71 you could be associated in business with him, but you must go ahead from now on, and Cathy must write no matter what, and neither of you must become discouraged. The work in one way or another is what will bring about the closeness you each desire, and you will have the help of an outsider who is a go-getter. Let this person, whoever he is, do whatever he can toward the goal. I don't mean to give up on Elvis, either.

There are those who can help you with both Tom and Elvis, so get their interest, and don't worry because Tom will eventually be all right. Hold Thanksgiving this year for his life and be thankful for the love you all have for one another, for I'm sure he was spared out of this love, because you all need him greatly. He has enriched all of your lives and that can never be lost no matter what, but his smile and his voice and his wit has been a blessing and will still be a comfort in time to come.

I'm all for Cathy for Elvis but I can well understand her love, your love, everyone else's love for this man. He's like a warm fire to stand before and warm oneself in the cold of the night that is sometimes life. So be thankful the fire still burns with its warmth, and you shall all have a closeness of spirit this Christmas. That is your great gift this Christmas, so let nothing take away from the love that you all share, and be happy in each other's happiness, even if you are apart.

Relay this message to Elvis, if in your own way or words, and let Cathy not be troubled; he is with her in heart, and shall be, as he is with you and close to Elvis, and the others he loves. Tom has found happiness within himself. Elvis and Cathy have yet to find it. But Tom's going to go on trying awfully hard to show them the way.

Tom didn't even mind the dying so much but that rebellious soul of his didn't like these kinds of goings on one bit. And, of course, you know who put him in this state. His lips will remain sealed, but he knows, he will never forget. His original injury would not have cost him this. She has great fear to face her husband, and don't think she doesn't. She knows, he knows, she saw his eyes and they said what words could never say in just a moment's time. I'll remain close and tell you as Tom progresses and his needs grow stronger in the next hours, days, or even weeks if need be.

Only Marlon must not drive for several hours after my visits through him. Thank you for your help,

Jeni

Marlon will soon receive confirmation of all I have said herein

Jeni Letter 3

This letter from Jeni was written shortly after it was discovered that Tom was still alive. She suggests helpful actions for Tom and Carmen. Curiously, Jeni admonishes Elvis to be "careful of his food all thru Dec." If this letter was written before Marlon sent the Sucaryl to a laboratory for analysis, Jeni's message may have prompted him to investigate the contents of the Sucaryl container.

(From Jeni)

Dear Carmelita;

Tom has been having a very rough time of it. His feelings have all awakened in the top half; his face and the back of his neck have given him unspeakable pain. Sounds have been coming back to his throat, but it is difficult for him to speak the words yet. He is shaky and uncertain, and the ordeal of the last two days has left him very weak.

By Thursday he will be getting the words out, the first real words may be forced out. After that he will get his voice back stronger as the pain subsides. He ought to reach this peak by late Wed. night your time, then when he finally falls asleep, the worst will be over. At least in this portion. Look for good news by Thurs. The pains should then gradually subside into aches that will ease each day. But still he cannot move from the waist down.

Perhaps another letter from you thru Elvis might help, once he is able to answer Elvis back. By about Fri. I would say. Even his manager is against another operation at this time, fearing to weaken him further. If nothing happens now it will mean waiting for him to get his strength back, then go thru more probing and tests back in London. And more time. If he got back the use of his legs now, he could be with his family in Wales by Xmas to recuperate there instead of in a hospital. His manager is going between there and London every other day now and it would be such a relief for all if Tom could lose what is keeping him down.

Also, Elvis must be very careful about drugs again, careful of his food all thru Dec.

Marlon's pen is running out and I am giving him trouble. Just pray for both tomorrow night, and I shall also be near.

Jeni

If you have a card or something to prove you are in the industry, it will come in very good use now. Harry was to tell you this some months ago but I don't know whether he did. Also—your presence will cheer him and raise his spirits so he will be able to more closely perceive any danger that may exist.

Jeni

Jeni Letter 4

It seems that Jeni is not above giving Carmen some practical business advice.

Dear Carmelita

This is Jeni here. It is not over yet for Tom. However, in one way, this may give you the break of keeping his manager here another couple of days. Things are changing too quickly to be able to tell you just what to do, but I can tell you a few things I know that if used wisely might be a help to you. Right now, Tom may be watched more closely than before, by the cut throats and police as well. So, you must not tip them off that you know Tom. Remember, anyone, anywhere could have a battery-operated microphone on their person. Get close if you can but be careful.

Be there no later than 2:30, and for some reason I feel you ought to try to call through to Tom or his manager right at 3 o'clock. Now, you may meet someone there who can help you. Don't let any grass grow under your feet. Take any opportunity, and if you can get near his manager, talk to him—but—charm him. What I mean is—he's all for Tom, yet he doesn't like overly pushy or efficient people. He wants—

or prefers—the people he deals with to also be concerned for Tom as well as for profit. You must show him you really care and believe in this property to bring out Tom's ability. He has turned down many profitable deals because of their strict commercial value. It's his business to look out for the money but he wants more than just that. He has to be made to want to deal with you.

Now, back to the someone who might help you. Take this help, and appreciate it, but don't let them use you. Beware if anyone offers you help to get to Tom for their own benefit. Take the help, you need it—but find another way to show appreciation. I liked the little girl, Debbie, last week. She reminds me a little of myself when I was young and full of hope. She may even be of valuable help to you. Also, Monday when you meet Tom's agent, there is one—someone—in the office you must befriend. Make it a point to befriend this person and stay in close contact, because they can help you next year. With tickets and with more direct help. Your best place to sit if you can arrange it is as far up front as possible on the left, on the aisle. Tom will sit there when talking to his guests, and you will be able to make closer contact as well as see from a vantage point. The front left aisle. And—Cathy has been very close to the breaking point - she must hold on a little longer. Monday could bring you good luck if properly handled.

If you only had a card you could send it with a note to Gordon Mills before the show (after 3) and ask if you could see him for just a minute after the taping. I'm sure you could get through with a card or a note from your mutual friend. But you need something. Work on these ideas, and when you move, move fast. Grasp all advantages or someone else will take them away from you.

If anything more comes to me I'll try to let you know. By the way—stay away from Mary—she's a nice girl but right now unstable. She knows she's a loser, and she's not thinking straight and this itself could lead Tom to trouble.

And tomorrow you don't need that. Cathy's already upset. You know what I mean. So just steer away for now at least. Nothing against the girl, Tom owes her something, but not what she wants now. She had her chance and he's in love for real now and neither he nor Cathy can afford to jeopardize that. I say that honestly, without bias.

Jeni

It is hard to resist the temptation to see the roots of Brando's later erratic and reclusive behavior in these "channeled" letters. And yet we know that millions of people believe in demons, angels, past lives, and communication with the deceased including channeling. We do not call these people lunatics or expect that mental illness will follow. What surprises me the most is that Marlon Brando, who I had always thought of as pragmatic and devoid of spiritual instincts or interests, would display a basic belief in God, religion, ghosts and other paranormal phenomena. Perhaps this illuminates the bond between him and Carmen Montez, a deeply spiritual woman, medium, and fellow believer with whom he honestly communicates his thoughts and experiences in confidence.

The Briefcase

My Elvis adventure had begun with the discovery of handwritten letters by Elvis and three other celebrities in three suitcases purchased at auction. It seemed nicely symmetrical, then, that a new Elvis adventure would begin with the discovery of more handwritten letters by the same celebrities in a briefcase hidden beneath a staircase.

I had always assumed that there were many more letters to Carmen than just those found in those blue suitcases. There are references to letters that were not in the collection, so it's possible some might have been lost or destroyed. Maybe some had been loaned out for reading by other parties, or even given to trusted friends for safekeeping. What if some of the letters had been stored in another box that was separated from the others? What if there had been four suitcases instead of three, but one previously had been sold? What if Carmen's written responses to Elvis are hidden away in some secret archive?

When preparing the manuscript of *Letters from Elvis* for publication, I hoped for three results: that many people would read the book and find it illuminating; that some readers would have information that could help me solve some unresolved mysteries; and, that if any other letters from the collection existed, the owners would contact me.

Bingo! Two months after publication, I got a phone call from a man who would only give me his first name—Brad. After I picked up the call, his voice faltered nervously as he said, "Is this Gary Lindberg?"

"Yes, that's me," I said warily, thinking it might be another death threat. My finger hovered over the disconnect button on my cell phone.

"I just read your book about the Elvis letters," Brad said. "Very nicely done."

My finger moved away from the red button. "Thank you."

What Brad said next was about to send me on another journey. "I think I have some more letters like the ones you wrote about."

"You mean letters to Carmen Montez?"

"Yes, I have quite a few."

I found this interesting, but I thought he was describing letters from some of Carmen's other students. Having access to such letters could help round out my understanding of this woman and how her other students interacted with her.

"Are the letters signed?" I asked. "Do you know who these letters are from?"

"Well—yes. They're signed by the same people who wrote your letters."

"You mean you have more letters from Elvis Presley to Carmen Montez?"

"I do… and from the others too."

"You mean Belafonte, Brando and Tom Jones?"

"Yes, from all of them."

I had already received several death threats from readers infuriated by what they judged to be my invasion of Elvis's privacy and the greed that had led me to brilliantly forge over a thousand pages of handwritten letters to make money off Elvis's good name. Ridiculous, of course, but my new wariness and increased cynicism caused me to doubt the authenticity of these new letters.

"You've seen some images of Elvis's writing in my book, and the others too," I said. "Does the handwriting in your letters look anything like my letters?"

"To my eye, absolutely," Brad replied. "My wife compared them too. Pretty sure they're the same writers. But you didn't have a lot of samples in your book."

"For legal reasons," I explained. "I'm thinking, though, that maybe you have copies of some of the letters I already have. Could be that Carmen made photocopies of some of them and you ended up with the copies."

"Don't think so," Brad said. "The paper isn't copy paper, and there's blue ink on some of the letters, not black. 'Course, there's color copiers out there, but none of these appear to be copies at all."

My enthusiasm was rising, so I tried to tamp it down with another challenge. "Brad, another good test would be for you to read a short passage from one of the Elvis letters, and I can see if those exact words appear in any of my letters. If they do, you have a photocopy."

All of the letters in my collection have been transcribed into a large Word file, so I can easily search for a phrase and find out if it existed in my document.

"OK," Brad said. "I've got an Elvis letter right here. It begins this way. 'I had to come back home on some business today, and I'm having a peanut butter sandwich with Marlon on the run.'"

"That's enough," I told him. "More than enough, actually." I searched my Elvis letters for "peanut butter sandwich with Marlon," a phrase that surely would appear nowhere else but in a letter from Elvis. Would I find it in my letters?

My heartbeat ramped up. "Don't have that. Let's try something from another letter."

"Try this, then. 'I can't perform anymore, night after night.'"

"Any punctuation I should know about?"

"Comma after anymore."

I searched.

"Again, nothing in my letters. Let's try a Brando letter."

"Give me a minute… OK, here's one. 'I've appointed myself temporary guardian of the mails.'"

I searched for "temporary guardian of the mails" and found nothing.

We continued for another five minutes, after which I was satisfied that his letters were not duplicates of the ones I had. "One more test, Brad, if you're game."

"Sure, this is exciting."

"Do you have a camera?"

"Sure, on my phone."

"I want you to take a picture of a page of one of the Elvis letters. Make sure you have good light on it—no shadows. Them email it to me." I gave him my personal email address.

A minute later I received that photo as an attachment. I had spent countless hours studying the handwriting in Elvis's letters; I knew it better than my own. The letter Brad had photographed was a dead-on match to the handwriting in my Elvis letters.

"Brad," I said, "how would you feel if I flew out to meet you?"

"Well, sure—I'm in Salt Lake City."

For some reason, I had thought he was in Los Angeles. That's where Carmen Montez had lived. I couldn't even imagine how Elvis's letters to Carmen had ended up in Salt Lake City. So I asked him.

Here is the amazing story.

Brad's Story

As a young man, Brad had dated a beautiful young woman whose parents owned an apartment building in Hollywood. I'll call her Sue Layton. Through frequent visits, he came to know and enjoy her older father and mother, and they thought he was a nice young man.

Unknown to Brad at the time, two individuals were renting apartments in the Layton's building. One of them was Carmen Montez and another was Carmen's ex-husband, a Cuban-Russian named George Ramentol. Though they had divorced, they remained friends and lived in separate apartments on the same floor.

Carmen Montez (left) with her husband George Ramentol (right) and a friend named Sybal around the time Carmen was Elvis's secret confidante. They are standing near the pool of Carmen's apartment on Carlton Way in Hollywood.

Carmen had divorced George because of his gambling. He had invested some of his winnings in Los Angeles parking lots, a notorious money laundering business for the mob. It was also likely that George was bipolar. Montez used the term "manic depressive."

After a time, Brad and Sue moved to Las Vegas, intending to get married there. But the urgency of a formal ceremony diminished, and the pressures of new jobs kept distracting them from legalizing their relationship.

One day, Carmen Montez passed away. Her husband, George, was not interested in her possessions, so the State of California put everything up for auction and Carmen Rayburn, her best friend, purchased the now-famous suitcases containing the celebrity letters. The Laytons leased the vacant apartment to another party, but George kept his unit.

On Tuesday, November 10, 1983, George climbed on his motorcycle to check on one of his parking lots. Suddenly, a car shot out of an alley and sideswiped him. Hit and run. Rumors circulated that it was a mob hit.

After the Laytons were notified that their tenant had died, the authorities took most of George's things for auction, and the Laytons cleaned out the rest of his apartment. But Mr. Layton remembered that George had occasionally tucked away a few things in a small storage space beneath the stairway. Inside that space they found a briefcase containing a lot of papers and some letters—nothing of apparent value. The Laytons hung onto the briefcase anyway. They had liked George Ramentol, at least during his "up" periods.

George Ramentol's briefcase, in which Brad discovered a trove of Carmen Montez's personal documents and more letters from Elvis and Marlon.

A short time later, Mr. and Mrs. Layton decided to retire. They sold their apartment building and moved into a manufactured home in Vegas to be near their daughter. Brad spent a lot of time with them, more time perhaps than he did with Sue Layton (Brad's relationship with Sue had become more distant).

Eventually, Brad and Sue broke up, but he stayed close to Sue's parents. They thought of Brad as a son, and when they both passed away, they left some of their things to him—including the briefcase, which he kept mainly for sentimental reasons, assuming it had no other value.

At some point, though—just as Carmen Rayburn had finally opened the suitcases she had bought at auction—Brad decided to go through the contents of the briefcase. A close inspection of the thirty letters stunned him. He knew he was in possession of something hugely significant.

Excitedly, he began the long and difficult journey of figuring out how to turn the letters into a book or a movie. He consulted attorneys and discovered the same legal quagmire that I did, a tangle of risks involving copyright problems, rights to privacy, and a mess of other problems. Setting the project aside, he went on with his life. He met and married his current wife and eventually was offered a job in Salt Lake City where he moved, briefcase in tow.

Having become a confirmed Elvis junkie, he found my book shortly after publication and read it in one night. "I was tingly," he told me, "because you had gone through the same frustrations I had—but you never gave up."

Salt Lake City

I arrived at Salt Lake City International Airport the afternoon of Monday, January 7, 2019. Brad picked me up and we drove immediately to his home, where he had offered to put me up until my Wednesday departing flight.

I met his beautiful wife, a member of the Cherokee Nation, who was actively researching her ancestry. We had a deep conversation about Elvis's belief that he was part Cherokee. The three of us stayed up late talking about our families, swapping stories about Elvis and diving more deeply into the story behind Brad's find.

Brad knew I was eager to look at the physical letters he possessed, so he brought them out. There was no doubt in my mind that his letters were genuine. They matched the letters in my collection perfectly. As I read through a few of them, I could see how the contents of Brad's letters consistently wove into the story threads contained in the Rayburn letters.

Two of the letters, however, excited me the most. The first was a letter from Priscilla Presley to Carmen that I had written about but was certain I'd never see. Marlon Brando had referred to it in one of his letters, but it was not in my collection. The second astonishing letter was from Elvis and described a vicious physical assault of which I was unaware. I will share transcripts of these letters later.

A few of the documents belonging to Carmen Montez that were found in her husband's briefcase.

The briefcase, it turned out, contained a wealth of personal documents that were immensely helpful in developing a better understanding of Carmen. I sifted through bank records for Carmen Montez and George Ramentol, which provided a history of financial activities and physical addresses; business correspondence, which shed light on Carmen's other professional activities; photographs of model and actor friends; and letters to Carmen from other "students" of her spiritual instruction.

Supplemented by evidence sent to me by other readers, I learned that Carmen Montez was not from Spain, as I had originally believed. She was born June 9, 1930, in Magdalena Jaltepec, a small town in the state of Oaxaca in southwestern Mexico. At the time of her birth, she had an eight-year-old brother, Vicente, and a two-year-old sister, Elena. Since there are no immigration records for her, it is possible she was an illegal immigrant.

Carmen seems to have had a well-equipped business mind as well as a profound spiritual intuition. From recently discovered documents, I learned that she had developed financing for a special project run by a large oil company. She founded and operated a talent agency representing models and actors. And we know from scores of celebrity letters that she was trying to establish a career as a movie producer by shopping a movie script to the industry with assistance from Harry Belafonte and Marlon Brando.

It is clear, though, from correspondence with her "students," that she had an uncanny ability to establish deep relationships and gain the trust of people she worked with. While she actively sought investments for projects she believed in, I have not come across any evidence that she conned anyone out of money or even requested payment for her spiritual counsel. Based on her bank records, she lived frugally with no large deposit spikes in her personal account.

I have had readers insist that Carmen Montez was a fictional creation and never existed. My research and the trove of personal records shared by Brad shows that Carmen was not only a real person, but quite a gifted one. Rather cruelly, skeptical readers have said that in photographs Carmen looks more like a man than a woman. Certainly, aging did her no great service, but her students' love and devotion as expressed in their letters suggests that her value to them was not based on physical beauty but rather on spiritual connection.

After completing a business transaction in which Calumet Editions and I secured the rights to Brad's story and the use of the materials contained in the briefcase for future book projects, we made high-resolution scans of everything and I took some pictures. Later, I recorded interviews with Brad.

On Wednesday, Brad took me to the airport, and I boarded a flight to Dallas with a short commuter flight to Tyler, Texas to spend a few days with a member of Elvis's close family who had contacted me after reading *Letters from Elvis*. Again, this book had introduced me to a chain of information and evidence about the Presley family that would have remained out-of-view except for the book's notoriety. Clearly, individuals knowledgeable about Elvis were finding the book credible and full of insights even as the so-called Elvis "experts," who believed the traditional folklore and manufactured PR about Elvis, were becoming inflamed by revelations of which they had no knowledge and had not blessed.

The next day, I traveled to Jefferson, Texas with the family member and his wife to photograph various sites where Elvis had spent time. I gave a printed copy of Priscilla's letter to the wife and asked her to read it aloud. As she did, I noticed tears in the eyes of my new friend as he drove.

"That's the Priscilla I know," he said. "Sounds just like her. All over the map emotionally. I wish Elvis could read this."

For me, finding this letter and its envelope is a miracle. Since I first learned about the letter, I have been obsessed with knowing what Priscilla could have written to her husband's secret confidante. I learned about Priscilla's note from an anecdote that Marlon Brando wrote to Carmen Montez, which I will repeat here for convenience:

I was coming back from this errand, approaching my house, and who should I see coming toward me but Priscilla. She had a cab waiting for her, informed me she and Lisa were on their way to Memphis and she had been looking for me. She shoved an envelope in my hand, smiled sweetly, and disappeared into the cab after telling me to give it to the "proper party." When I looked at it, it was addressed as you see, and she was gone. So—I didn't know what else to do, other than give it to you. I'm anxiously waiting for word from you. Please let me know if there's anything I have to do. I know where Elvis will be tonight, and I can telephone his trailer if it's anything urgent. I've been puzzled and rather upset all day. Let me know.

Marlon

Now, for the first time, and since no response was ever received after our estoppel letters were sent to the relevant parties, including Priscilla Presley, my publisher has agreed to print a transcription of the entire text of Priscilla's six-page letter to Carmen Montez.

Priscilla's Letter to Carmen Montez

This is the front of the envelope that Priscilla handed Marlon outside his home. When handing it to him, she said, "Give it to the proper party." The blue-green envelope was addressed: *To Elvis' "Sister"* and marked *Personal*. Apparently, Priscilla knew that her husband called Carmen "Sis" or "Sister" in his correspondence, which Priscilla could only have known if she had seen drafts of his letters or if he had told her this detail. Since Elvis had been careful to keep his relationship with Carmen secret, I think the latter is unlikely.

The front of the envelope in which Priscilla enclosed her letter to Montez.

The back of Priscilla's envelope shows marks where she had taped the flap as an added precaution that no one but Carmen could open it undetected and read her message.

The back of the envelope in which Priscilla enclosed her letter to Montez.

As a salutation to Carmen, Priscilla begins her letter with the words *Dear "Sister-in-law"*. After all, if Carmen were Elvis's "sister," then she would be Priscilla's "sister-in-law."

Priscilla's handwritten salutation to Carmen Montez.

To call attention to her little joke, she follows up this salutation with: "Is this what I call you? I'm still uncertain." Priscilla may also be implying that she understands the intimacy that exists between Elvis and Carmen, perhaps even envies the depth of their "sibling" relationship as an in-law sometimes does. I think perhaps she is also confessing a suspicion that the relationship is more than platonic.

Here is the full text of Priscilla's letter to Carmen Montez. It is an accurate word-for-word transcription except for the paragraphing that I have added for readability. The original letter was written mostly in a single unbroken paragraph on six sheets from edge-to-edge with no margins.

> Dear "Sister in law"
>
> Is this what I call you? I'm still uncertain. You must excuse the lack of protocall [protocol] and pretty paper, the informality. There is much to write and little space or time. Yet if I saw you face to face I couldn't talk. It's like going to confession this way. I need help, for my husband's sake if not for mine. I don't know how this help will come, but I've been half out of my mind. Elvis is too much for me to handle. I need help to let go of him. I want to but something in me won't let me and it's horrible the way we're hurting each other.
>
> I wanted to kill him the other night so nobody else would ever have him. No that is not entirely true. I couldn't bear to kill him. But I wanted to hurt him more than he's hurt me. I

wanted to twist something down into his guts and twist it and twist it and only then, if I could hurt him more than he's hurting me, could I forgive him. Then I'd feel sorry for him, pity him enough to forgive him. Only by then Elvis would hate me. I swear I'm going to do it if something doesn't take this feeling out of me. There must something terrible in me that he brings out.

I'm doing a miserable thing to him right now. I'm taking him apart to you. I'm not allowing him the grace of privacy. But I'm doing it, though he would hate me, the demons in me may be appeased. If they are not I fear for him and for myself. Elvis creates in me a terrible state of confusion. My feeling for him changes from second to second. I can't describe my confusion unless I describe the changing of my feelings. And they go back to him.

For a little while I thought I was getting close to him. I've grown up enough in the past year to see through the surface glamour of his image. But I still don't know who he is, what he is, or how to reach him. He changes from moment to moment. He is sunshine and green fields, he is thunder and storm. He's a boy, younger than I am, and then he's a man. He is sweetness, kindness, tenderness, beyond belief. Then he is a savage, filled momentarily with the very violence he hates. Sometimes he's aloof, fighting me with all his power as though he's afraid to love. He's naive, then he's honest and open and forgiving, coming to me in forgiveness and his own free will. He is warm, tender, with gentle hands and wet lashes touching my cheek. Other times he is intense, burning, with the grace of an Indian, wild, abandoned, strong.

And now there is this, these other women. [Before this letter was written, three women had filed paternity suits against Elvis, including Patricia Parker, no relation to Col. Tom Parker.] And the thought of him with them is driving me crazy. I thought I could do what I wanted to do. I never dreamed he would do this. [Clearly, Priscilla believes the charges made against Elvis.] I wish he were a homosexual now. Yes, I've broken away from his image, but I can't get past that which my hands can touch. When I try to find Elvis his body keeps getting in my way.

I don't know who he is, what he is. That night he opened in Las Vegas last January, he was so cold to me. Even in his aloofness I've never known him to be cold. Child-like, but not cold or unresponsive. Afraid, but never icy. It's the only time I failed to get a response from him. Now I know why. It was that girl he wanted then, not me. [Priscilla appears to be referring to Patricia Parker.] It burns me to remember that coldness in him. Elvis may have told you about that terrible fight we had a couple of weeks ago when this came out. Three law-suits. Three. He can't say anything to me after this.

I was ready two weeks ago to take him for every penny he has, to take our daughter away where he would never see her, to never let him see the baby when it comes. [Priscilla confirms here a post-Lisa Marie pregnancy that was never made public.] I don't know why I didn't. Instead I started covering for him. I don't know why. I started being seen around him so people would think things were good with us despite all this. I lied and smiled. But as much as I wanted him to tell me it was all a lie, he wouldn't. I was ready for his lies but he never spoke them, never tried to reassure me. When I asked him he looked at me funny and turned his back. I thought "at least he's not lying".

But strangely, the thing that disappointed me about him was his fighting that Parker girl. He tried to deny my child, now he's doing the same thing to her. I gave Elvis more credit for kindness and responsibility than he's shown. If he'd own up to his mistakes, I could forgive him. He went right from me to her the very next day.

I keep trying to tell myself that was January and I'd given him a bad time, making fun of him in public at his opening.

After the fight we had, Elvis and I didn't talk to each other, not until last Tuesday, a week. I went to the show to be seen there that night, and afterwards I got stuck talking to friends from Memphis, and by that time Elvis had gone upstairs to the suite to rest between shows. I went up to tell him I realized that was then and this was now, and I felt that was why he came to me that night a couple of months ago, before the awful ordeal, with tenderness and forgiveness for me, the night I knew I loved him. But I never got to say it to him. He was in the shower when I went in. He came out a little later without anything on but his rings. I started out all wrong, jumping at him for coming out in the nude. It could have been his Aunt or anyone else instead of me. His attitude was aloof. He said "sorry, I just didn't expect anybody else to be in my bedroom." I felt angry again. He was buckling on his wristband and finally he relented and asked how I was feeling. Suddenly, I went crazy looking at him. The anger was gone, nothing else mattered. I forgot pride, I even forgot I was pregnant. [Priscilla is confirming an event that is covered in detail in my book *Letters from Elvis*.]

Elvis has, to me, the beautiful body of an Indian, he's one man who should never even wear clothes. Even the briefest? of trunks cuts his body lines, while without clothes he's graceful and beautiful as no man I've known. Pale tan all over, with beautiful skin, firm and soft all at once. His hands so sensitive, and his muscles and veins aren't the knotty kind of the burly man, but smooth and sleek as an Indians beneath his skin. Most people, taking him apart, assume that it's his movements that make him sexy. That, too, but I think one of the sexiest things about him is his face. He doesn't have to put it on, it's there. His rib cage runs into his waist line and his hips are straight on the sides, which gives him little waistline, but, oh, in the back, he's so rounded and firm and his stomach is taut, seductive and where it counts he's got it.

Elvis doesn't wear his clothes too tight like some performers do, and some of those girls who try to stare through his clothes would be surprised at how voluptuous he really is. He wasn't nicknamed "Elvis the Pelvis" for nothing. He would hate me right now for saying that. I don't know why I enjoy humiliating him.

My feelings all changed so rapidly after that. I was staring at him, angry with an anger that kept me from saying the things I'd come to say. Suddenly I wasn't angry, I couldn't talk. Before I knew what I did I went to him. He tried to squirm away from me. He told me to cool it, he had to go on in little more than an hour. He kept telling me to cut it out. Then he made me cry. But that always gets him and he melted and put his arm around me. He said he was sorry, he didn't mean it that way, he was just tired, tense and jumpy. He said he had to keep away from me because it would be harmful to me with the baby due in another month and what had happened a while ago. He said it would hurt and he didn't want to hurt me. He had enough on his mind he said.

I didn't care. All I cared about right then was making love to my husband, but my husband is a prude sometimes. He believes in a two-way deal or nothing. I finally seduced him, and I must say he is always kind and considerate, even when he gets a little away from himself. But the other night he was something else. For a while I was frightened. Elvis is stronger than he looks, but I've never been afraid of his strength. One moment I loved him – he was beautiful and awesome and magnificent. The next moment I lashed out at him – he was savage, fearsome, frightening – all this at one time. He was terrible and still he was beautiful. He hurt me and I clawed at him and screamed for him to stop but he couldn't. His stomach muscles were tight and his whole body was taut and it was like clawing at stone. For a minute it was terrible. He came at me with such terrible drive, shoulders thrown back – and – God, I've seen him pretty wild sometimes, but not like that. I thought he'd turn himself inside out.

But suddenly I opened my eyes and I looked onto his face – and it's very hard to explain, but his face was beautiful. It was twisted by the moans trying to come from his throat – but he had the beauty of a storm – of lightning and thunder and as I watched his face I thought all the hurt was gone. The mental as well as the physical. And I so much wanted it to be all gone. I wanted to swallow him up in entirety, to draw him in with our child and give him the rebirth of body and soul or whatever, no matter the pain or consequence. It was as though he wanted just that. I truly cared only about nothing more than what I could give to him right then.

Then he fell into my arms limp as a rag doll, trembling all over and mumbling that he didn't know what happened to him. He was a very little boy again and I loved him dearly. Finally he was breathing again and the trembling subsided into sleep. And there, feeling warm and happy the old devil came back into me again. I wondered if he was like that with her. I thought "maybe she loved him, too, and he turned on her".

I saw a scissors lying on the night table. I let go of Elvis with one hand and I picked it up. All I know is I wanted to rip open his stomach. As quickly as I loved him I turned to hating him. I accidentally woke him, touching the cold points against his stomach. He woke with such a start I could feel his heart leap up in his chest. When he saw it was only me he closed his eyes again. But he must have caught the look on my face because a second later his eyes flew open and his hand moved down there.

Somewhere a voice was saying "kill him, 'kill him," and out loud I was saying no, no, no and he was looking at me like I was crazy. He pushed the scissors away with his hand and got up, looking at me like that – without a word, just shaking his head. I heard myself telling him nobody else was going to have him. I don't remember too much of what he said then.

I do remember he said I always killed everything good. I got him backed against the casing of the bathroom door. That's the first time he ever spoke about the girl. He said he never laid eyes on her. But with the scissors pressed against him, how could I believe what he said? The strange thing is – that wasn't me there – because I don't want Elvis that way. I don't want to hurt him. No matter what I've done, or what he's done, I don't want to hurt him. Truly. Please believe this.

Now, counting this – I'm even glad he did wrong. Now we're on even terms. Besides – he's going to live his life, and I'll live mine. And if neither one of us love anyone else, and we meet now and then and find enough love or fondness to give each other – that is how it will be. I don't want anymore hurts.

Anyway, at that moment, Dee and Vernon came into the outside room and in that moment Elvis pushed past the scissors and got into the bathroom and locked the door. I saw a bloody scratch across his hip bone and front but I don't think I really hurt him. But I can't say what would have happened if Vernon and Dee had not come in. I don't understand this terrible compulsion to hurt him while at the same time I fear for his life.

The baby's due soon and after that we'll have to stay apart. There are things I want without Elvis. It's dangerous for me to get pregnant again and every time I am around him and I'm not pregnant he's managed to accomplish it. So this time I'm going to stay away far away. But I hate myself for what I've done, and I still have great fear for Elvis' life. And for my own. If you can understand him better than I can, then do whatever you can for him. And I'm sorry it has to be this way.

Whatever happens I don't want to hurt him anymore.

Priscilla

Elvis, Priscilla and daughter Lisa Marie in 1970.

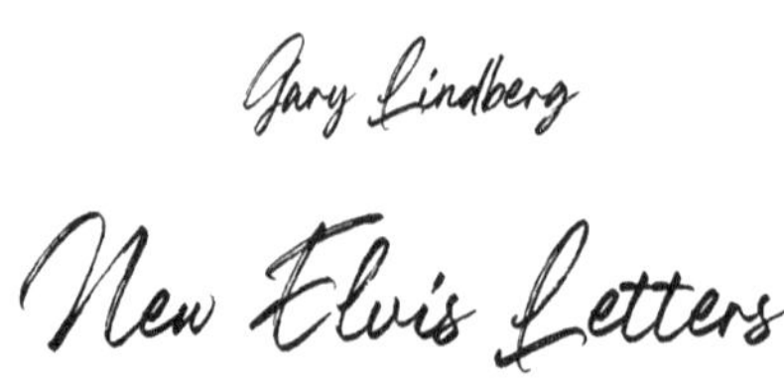

In George Ramentol's briefcase, Brad had found thirty letters, seven from Elvis to Carmen. In a thirteen-page handwritten letter, previously unknown to me, Elvis describes in detail yet another abduction and episode of torture. I have not been able to precisely date this letter, but I believe it was delivered to Carmen a little more than a year after Marlon's letter of March, 1970, in which he wrote a postscript as follows:

> P.S. Carmen—for a week now—I've had a funny—a strange, nameless fear for Elvis. I don't know what it is, but I'm afraid of something. I wish you knew what it might be.

A transcript of this letter is risky for Calumet Editions to publish because of numerous issues, as outlined in *Letters from Elvis* (pages 129-135). The letter appears to implicate Colonel Tom Parker, Elvis's longtime manager, in collaborating with the mob to either punish Elvis or even possibly kill him.

Here, for the first time, is the newly found letter from Elvis, written mid-July 1971.

The simple envelope, with Carmen's name, in which Elvis enclosed a letter about Colonel Parker's association with the mob.

The Elvis "mob" letter to Carmen showing ink bleed-through. Opening page is on the right-hand side.

Dear Carmen:

I'm feeling pretty bad; shaking, and my head's killing me. Marlon scrounged up some paper to write on in the office as I couldn't have gotten up to get some. I don't know how I'm going to open in Tahoe tomorrow. I don't know what hit me this time. I'm still dazed. I know I came home and I was feeling pretty good but tired. I let my driver go home to his wife, and my other boys had left from San Bernadino's to go to Tahoe. [Elvis is scheduled to perform his first series of shows at the Sahara in Lake Tahoe July 2 to August 2, 1971. Dad and Dee were upstairs. I'd gone up to speak to him [Vernon] but he was snoring so I came back down to the kitchen to get something to eat.

I'd made a peanut butter sandwich and I'd just started to

pour a glass of milk when something hit me on the head, then there was something evil smelling over my face, and the next thing I knew I was in my own driveway and someone was pulling me out of my navy blue Cadillac. I was dazed but I turned on them. I still had all my rings on so I got in quite a showing for myself. I put up a good fight and I got back in the car and I rammed it into the front gate hard but the force threw me so hard that with ordinary glass I'd of been through the windshield. Instead, I banged the right side of my head, again, on the glass.

After that I remember very faintly being dragged into my house. I picked up snatches of a phone conversation here and there between blackouts. There were three men and a girl, and they seemed to be talking to Parker [Elvis's manager, Col. Tom Parker]. Unless I was hallucinating. It seemed like he wanted no part of it. They put the phone down one time and walked away while he was talking. I heard him tell them to let me go and I heard him say he was sorry he ever got into "this thing."

They said they couldn't let me go now, it was too late, and they wouldn't return "the money." He must have said to keep it and then said that I was dangerous to them now. They weren't worried about him "keeping his mouth shut" because he was strongly implicated.

I blacked out and woke up when I was being dragged out behind my house. There's an old bridle path that isn't used anymore. It's down in the back and runs down behind Barbra Streisand's house on the way to Sunset Blvd. It's all grown over and very secluded. They tied me hand and foot to a tree there, with rawhide, and they started debating on how to get rid of me. One of them didn't like the idea of using the gun and they'd just about decided to use a knife on me when the girl chickened out.

She said she didn't want to be there when they did it and then one of them had a length of rawhide left over. He soaked it in a flask he had in his pocket and knotted it around my throat. He said they'd leave me there while the rawhide dried and then they'd come back and get rid of my body. When rawhide dries it gets tighter and tighter and I'd choke to death while it shrank.

They'd then planned to set fire to me and the whole brush area back there to destroy all evidence. They left me there and for two hours I slowly started choking. The rawhide was biting into my wrists and had started cutting into my throat. I couldn't breathe. I couldn't even pray because it took everything I had left in me to try to get some air.

It was a horrible two hours. I finally gave up and I felt myself slipping away from the daylight into blackness. The next thing I know I was on the ground and Marlon and Dad Presley and Joe Esposito were working on me. I couldn't talk for a long time. I'm only whispering now and I'm wondering about singing tomorrow night. I'm sore, my back and shoulders ache, and my ribs feel like they're broken. But the worst is my throat and the tendonitis has flared up again and it is a very painful ailment.

My face had been black and blue but I guess it's starting back to normal color now, although my neck is raw and so is my wrist and my head feels like somebody took it off and played football with it. I've got quite a bump on the right side, and again in back. My hair covers it but I can't put my head down only on the left side.

Please pray for me Wed. night. Right now I think I'm about to be somewhat ill so a quick goodbye.

El

P.S.: This isn't really a P.S., it's more of a continuation and an exercise to get my wrists circulating again. There's something I keep thinking about. These guys are definitely not the same kind I've come up against before. They were very smooth, more businesslike. Except for the girl. They weren't interested in me in the way the others were. Only the girl. I'm trying to figure out where she fits in. She had very long fingernails, bright red, with American flag decals on. She took my belt off and stuck it in her handbag for a "souvenir" while the guys weren't watching. She kept playing with the zipper on my jump suit, zipping it up and down, and running her fingers over the scar on my left shoulder where Sol Stingers burned me making Charro.

I must admit I played up to her thinking she would untie me. She became quite amorous and I told her, "Honey, I can't do anything with my hands tied" but there was no way she would untie me and then I blacked out again, I think from the two bumps on my head.

Parker is here. He just pulled into my driveway. I told him on the phone a little while ago to "get his kids on over here" and I didn't expect him to show up but he's here. I'll tell you about it after he leaves.

___ [A long line occurs here indicating that the following message was written later, I believe.]

Well, I really had it out with Col. Parker! I finally said everything I wanted to say to him. He walked in and I showed him my bruises and my hands and my neck, and I asked him why he did this to me. He looked at me strangely and he said "You know?" I said yes, I know.

He touched my neck and he sat down and put his hands over his face and I really let into him. I pulled no punches, I held nothing back. He said he tried to stop it. I said I knew that but why did he do it in the first place? He said he needed the money, and I said why didn't he come to me and ask me for it if he needed it so badly.

He said he thought he'd be doing me a favor because I'd wanted to die. He didn't think I cared about living anyway and I told him that was my decision to make not his. I'm tired of being stalked and living in fear. He said when I seemed to pull out of my mood of several years ago he tried to call them off. He said when I'd become ill he told them to hold off. Then he cried and he said he was an old man.

I said "But I'm not." I've got thirty-five years to catch up with you, and when I die I want it to be between God and me."

He swore to me he was not behind those other attacks [by the Katzman gang] and he warned me "Look out for yourself, boy, because they're afraid you'll identify them now." And I know that's true.

I do expect the girl to show up again somehow. She wanted me so badly she would have done anything except go against them to their face. I don't quite know what to do if she shows up again. I'm not sure how I'll handle that. I'm thinking, if she's tipped her hand to them they just might get rid of her. They're very professional, very thorough, wiping off fingermarks, etc. She goofed them up a little, and what I'm wondering is how they'd allow a woman to get in the way. I think she was the boss's girlfriend. Nevertheless, I can't figure it.

To get back to Parker, I told him I'd fire him if I legally could, and I ended up loaning him half a million dollars. I don't know why I did it, Carmen, unless – well, I guess, heck, it's better to get it all out in the open than to go around like this. As much as I knew he was behind it – it's a hard thing to explain – I felt pangs of real hurt when it came to the showdown.

He just didn't know what to say when I wrote out the check. Maybe God told me to turn the other cheek or maybe it's something in myself that had to show him how foolish it all was. I handed him the check and I said "Now see how easy it was. You never had to try to kill me for it."

He asked me to forgive him. I know you're supposed to forgive and forget. To forgive without forgetting is not forgiving at all. But I'd be a hypocrite if I said it wouldn't take me quite some time to try.

Meanwhile my life is still in jeopardy. I know, Carmen, there have been times when I've felt my life has not been worth living. I know what I am. One day not too long ago I had a good talk with God. I said "Lord, I know what I am. Sometimes I'm selfish, sometimes I do things that hurt others who love me. But I've never meant to hurt anyone. That's why you've got to help me to be strong and overcome this thing that's been eating away at me."

I did something nobody knows about last Jan. It was between me and the Lord. That's why I mean it when I say "my soul's in Your hands." I couldn't stand myself when I looked in the mirror. My face was all swollen. I didn't care when I worked. Now, I'm coming back to myself. My weight is down and even though I still have the health problems, I feel more alive, and I'm once more aware of the world around me.

Of people, I can accept love and at least try to give it. But I know it's time, they're as much or more afraid of me now as I am of them. I've got to do something about it and the old Colonel's afraid, too. I feel strangely sorry for him. A few months ago I couldn't have felt sorrow. It's funny. Anyway, that's the way it is right now. I know your love is with me, but what am I to do from a practical stand-point?

Push things with him now, please. This may make a difference in his viewpoint and his dealings. Or with his conscience. He seems to have one.

Elvis

P.P.S.

He just called me. Parker. He said not to worry, he'd go to Tahoe with me and stay with me every minute, even sit out in front. I told him in the first place how in hell did he expect me to sing decently in the condition my throat was in, and secondly, for once in my life I was going to tell him what to do! I said he could come up with me, it would be expected, but after I opened I wanted him to get his hide out of there and back here to L.A. because I didn't want to have to look at him for ten days.

I feel sick enough! Besides, I want him back here so you can work on him. For one time I may be doing a bit of the bossing around here for a change. From now on, if I live long enough, I may have things a little bit more my way!! I've had it, Carmen.

I've had it!

One moment I could sit down and cry and knock my head against the wall, and the next I'm mad! I'm burning up right now. In fact, I think I'm going to smash up a few things. I have a terrible temper when I let it go. I haven't felt like this since I smashed up a jukebox in Tennessee. I was mad at myself then. I broke my hand taking it out on a brick doing karate another time. But I've just had it and that's it!

Man, am I sore! I don't know when or how I'll eat. I can't hardly swallow liquid.

A fan photo of Elvis performing in his "cobweb" jump suit in the High Sierra Room at the Sahara Tahoe on opening night, July 20, 1971, a few days after being attacked at home by the mob.

This next letter from Elvis is a follow-up to the last one. I suspect, though, that a missing letter may have been sent to Carmen between these two because Elvis refers to something he expects Carmen to know. While performing Tahoe near the end of his Sahara show schedule, he sees the mob girl "down front" in the audience. He must have told Carmen that when he was assaulted he was wearing the gold cross he commonly wears around his neck, and it was taken from him. The "girl" shows it to him and then gives him names of several influential people behind the attack.

Here is the letter Elvis had delivered to Carmen along with his latest single, "Life."

Dear Carmen;

I hope you will like the record. I wrote it one day last January – it was really pretty much the way I felt and what I said to God, and I just put it down the way I felt it. And I promised I would acknowledge him in the way I do best – so I made it part of my performance and somehow I feel better when I'm working now. I feel like I'm closer to him.

The girl [from the mob] was here in Tahoe, Carmen. I didn't get my cross back – not yet, anyway – but I learned the names of her accomplices, and I was about to find out who they were working for – Parker had hired someone to hire them – and I wanted his name – when Marlon goofed me up trying to help me. He doesn't seem to realize I'm a big boy and I can handle one woman by myself.

I spotted her down front Sunday night [at the Sahara Tahoe during his performance] and she held up the cross to show she had it. I let her come backstage and she pulled a gun on me. I finally got her to put the gun away and she reminded me she had actually saved my life, or they'd have killed me on the spot, and she said she had come back later, as soon as she could get away, to cut me loose. It must have been the truth because she had the cross.

She came back the next night [to Elvis's subsequent performance] and she told me her name was Karen, and she didn't hold a gun on me this time. She gave me the names of the others, and they're all well-to-do or of prominent families. If anything happens to me I'm going to give you these names. Her boyfriend is named Walter Breckner, and he's a big-wig stock broker. Another is Joseph Lewis, and he is the son of Loretta Young's [a famous actress'] former husband. Another is Lou Van de Kamp of the restaurant family.

I didn't tell anyone else, not Marlon even, because if they ever found out my source they'd kill the girl. And while I'll admit she should be dealt with by the proper authorities, I wouldn't want her killed because of me. She's a dangerous chick, but man is she put together! Under other circumstances – well, anyway, she said if I'd let her come back the next night she would tell me who they work for. She hinted that I might be surprised who sets up such things.

She wanted something from me and I wanted to find out

from her, and under the circumstances I was getting the best of the deal – and she was just about where I wanted her – when detective Brando jumped out of a closet, scared me half to death because I thought it was one of them, and she took off out an open window, and I never even got my cross back and I'll bet she never shows again either.

I was so frustrated I could have choked him with my red scarf. Now I don't know if I'll ever know. I can handle her but I can't handle all of them single-handed. I knew perfectly well what I was doing and if Marlon had let me handle it I'd know by now who I have to look out for. Now that it's in the open I know I can expect anything and I have to be ready. Not only for myself, Carmen, but others – such as Lisa [Marie] could be in danger as well, if they happened to be around at the wrong time.

I knew what I was doing but Marlon thinks I've lost my head and it's enough to make a saint cuss. I know what was on the girl's mind when she saved me, but the fact remains I wouldn't be here today if she hadn't, and she did take a chance to tell me what I tell you here. Remember those names, just in case, but only in case of an emergency – if anything happens to me or if the life of anyone dear to me should be in danger and I'm somewhere where I can't help.

I'm so sore, Carmen, I feel like I've been run over by that steam roller I sing about! The first night I opened I slid down into the split and then couldn't get up without Charlie Hodges' help! I haven't tried it since, and I bow only from the waist up.

Parker left. I couldn't stand his presence and I told him to go and leave me in peaceful misery. Asserting oneself is very great for the soul, Carmen. Well, I have to get this to Marlon before he goes to sleep.

Take care of yourself till I get back.

Loving you, Elvis

Reasons to Get Away?

The correspondence on which I based *Letters from Elvis* and this book provides ample evidence that Elvis had a difficult, frightening and painful life, one for which fame and fortune did not begin to compensate. He faced abductions, torture, sexual abuse, poisonings, betrayals, stalking, infidelity, panic attacks, exhaustion and multiple fears and phobias. I'm certain we don't yet know the whole story.

No wonder he at times considered suicide. As Colonel Parker said after the assault in 1971, Elvis seemed unhappy with life and anxious to die, so what difference would it make if he did?

Conspiracy theorists who believe Elvis faked his death to get away from the pressures of being a star don't really understand how terrible his life was. There has been chatter about the mob being after him and about him no longer being able to tolerate the celebrity lifestyle. What most people have not understood is that it was not so much his public life but his *private* life that was hell on earth. In hindsight, the cobweb jump suit he wore opening night at the Sahara Tahoe in 1971 seems symbolic of the malicious web he had been caught in and from which he could not escape.

I don't doubt that he wanted to fake his death to end it all. He was surrounded by stress and sorrow with no end in sight. The only surprising thing is that he made it to 1977 before… what? An overdose, a heart attack, a secret flight out of Memphis?

Gary Lindberg

My mission has been to illumine the harsh life of an immensely talented entertainer, a spiritual seeker, a forgiving soul, and a courageous man who somehow kept making legions of fans intensely happy while he suffered largely alone. My respect for him has grown with each letter I've read.

Since discovering Brad's briefcase full of insights and being invited into the "family," I now see a pathway to the rest of the true story which has only begun to be told—

Stay tuned.

Acknowledgements

This book would not exist if not for my partner and publisher Ian Graham Leask at Calumet Editions. This unique sequel to Letters from Elvis, containing the verbatim text of Marlon Brando's letters to Carmen Montez, was his idea, and he recommended it with the courage of is conviction knowing the significant legal issues surrounding this project.

There are numerous others to acknowledge as well, including the staff at Calumet, my son Scott, my sister Bonnie, copyeditor Rick Polad, friend and compatriot in the Elvisphere Guy Cooper, and many early readers who guided the writing process with their insights and encouragement.

A special thank you goes out to Jonathon Kirsch, our literary attorney, whose foresight in guiding the complex legal process on *Letters from Elvis* proved to help enable the publishing of the text of Marlon Brando's letters.

About the Author

Gary Lindberg spent forty years as a filmmaker and the last twelve years writing and publishing books. As an author, he has written four consecutive Amazon #1 bestselling novels: *The Shekinah Legacy*; *Sons of Zadok*; *Deeper and Deeper*; and *Ollie's Cloud*. He wrote a previous book about Elvis Presley entitled *Letters from Elvis*. With his mother, Elayne Lindberg, he co-authored a nonfiction book entitled *The Power of Positive Handwriting*. He is the co-founder of Calumet Editions, a publisher of fiction and nonfiction.

As a filmmaker, he has written, produced and/or directed countless corporate films, TV commercials, music videos and entertainment movies. He co-wrote and produced *That Was Then, This Is Now*, a Paramount feature film starring Emilio Estevez and Morgan Freeman. He has won over one hundred national and international awards for his work in media, including two Grand Awards from the New York International Film Festival.

www.ingramcontent.com/pod-product-compliance
Lightning Source LLC
Chambersburg PA
CBHW031950080426
42735CB00007B/339

* 9 7 8 1 9 5 9 7 7 0 8 3 1 *